superstitions, old wives' tales, & folklore

Cind

Table of Contents

Chapter 1: Farm Lore
    Chapter 2: Birds and Insects
    Chapter 3: Man's Best Friend
    Chapter 4: The Fantastic Feline
    Chapter 5: Household Superstitions
    Chapter 6: We Should Be So Lucky
    Chapter 7: Cemeteries & Funerals
    Chapter 8: Pregnancy and Motherhood
    Chapter 9: Venturing Into the Darkness
    Chapter 10: An Odd Hodgepodge of Beliefs
    Chapter 11: Witches in Lore
    Chapter 12: The Human Body
    Chapter 13: Love, Sweet Love
    Chapter 14: Vampire Lore
    Chapter 15: Old Wives' Tales Involving Food
    Chapter 16: The Mythology of Wolves
    Chapter 17: Strange Beliefs about Animals
    Chapter 18: Oldies, But Goodies
Sources
Acknowledgements
Copyright/Publishing

Introduction

I was blessed to have been born into a family whose members, though not always in agreement, are open to just about anything. This includes God, the devil, ghosts, angels, superstitions, folklore and nearly everything in between; all of which were as real to them as the earth and sky.

Having been raised to always keep an open mind, I learned early on that few things are out of the realm of possibility. It was that philosophy that inspired this book. Within these pages you will find samplings of well-known bits of lore with which you are probably familiar, as well as several obscure beliefs and customs you may be learning of for the first time.

Let it be known that a small fraction of these have made appearances in some of my previous works. They are included here, not only because any collection pertaining to these subjects would be lacking without them, but also because, alas, not everyone reads everything I write.

With that said, I hope you enjoy this glimpse into the world of superstitions, old wives' tales, and folklore, a magical place where nothing is ever as it seems.

Chapter 1:

Farm Lore

Most of us have, at one time or another, cracked open an egg only to find a spot of blood on the yolk. While this is not unusual and certainly doesn't affect the quality of the product, some find the sight a bit off-putting. On the farm that my uncle used to own and operate, depending on the amount of blood that was present; this naturally occurring phenomena indicated that something evil had paid a visit.

He believed that the presence of blood in an egg, or fresh milk, was the result of the animals involved having seen the devil. Apparently, the shock of finding themselves in the company of this most sinister of beings pollutes their systems, causing blood to be present in anything they produce. Fortunately for the farmer, the effects are only temporary. Within a few days, the traumatized livestock get over the encounter and everything returns to normal.

Though the farmer at the center of the following true account didn't go so far as to blame the devil for the bizarre events that befell his operation, the similarities between what he experienced and my uncle's unconventional beliefs are frighteningly obvious.

Growing up, we had an 'egg man' who delivered farm fresh produce to our home every week. There was a time, however, when he halted his activities, forcing my mother to purchase our eggs from a local supermarket. It was only later on that we learned the reason for the interruption in service.

After the episode had blown over, the egg man's wife, who happened to be a close friend of my mother's, shared with her that their troubles had started one night when her husband heard strange noises coming from the chicken coop. Fearing that a predator had found its way into the enclosure, he had grabbed his shotgun and headed out to investigate.

The closer he got to the area where the birds were housed, the more worried he became. By that time, not only were the chickens carrying on, but some of the other farm animals had joined in as well. Before long, he would learn the alarming reason for their distress.

As the farmer approached the pen, a man he could not identify had bolted from within and taken off running through the pasture. Even though the trespasser was already retreating, the egg man had fired off a shot to warn him against ever coming back.

The animals eventually settled down and, thinking that the ordeal was over, the farmer went back inside. The next morning, he would see something that caused him to suspect that the stranger's appearance may have been more ominous than it seemed.

When he went to collect the eggs, he could tell right away that something wasn't right. He had two basic forms of quality control that he regularly utilized. One was to sample the product for himself. The other was to hold the specimens up to a light to make sure that the contents were uniform.

On that occasion, when he held the first egg in front of the lamp, rather than viewing the pristine product he strived for, he found himself staring at a dark blotch that had formed inside the shell. His curiosity piqued, he cracked the egg and watched as a glob of what appeared to be coagulated blood oozed from inside.

Hoping that this was a fluke, he inspected the eggs that had been collected from the other hens. To his dismay, they were the same as the first one. In somewhat of a panic, he began cracking the eggs into a bucket. Instead of boasting yellow yolks and clear whites, every last one of them consisted almost entirely of blood.

After contacting his customers and explaining to them that he would be unable to make his deliveries that week, the egg man had set about trying to find out what had caused the events that, if they continued for very long, would put his family in the poorhouse.

His first thought had been that the feed had somehow become tainted, but after going through it with a fine-tooth comb, he determined that it was of superior grade. Ultimately, he could find nothing to account for what had been present inside the eggs.

Several days went by with little improvement. The hens that were still laying were producing only one or two eggs each, none of which were edible. To make a bad situation even worse, one of his prized dairy cows went into labor prematurely, resulting in her calf being stillborn.

A week or so later, the storm passed and things returned to normal. Deliveries resumed and all was well. According to his wife, the farmer never did find out what was behind the strange happenings that had threatened to destroy everything they had built. The fact that the first bloody eggs were discovered the morning after the stranger appeared was glossed over for reasons that were never quite clear. In the end, one has to wonder who the mysterious prowler was and what, if any, role he played in the events that followed.

Back in the day, finding a snake in the well water was not an unheard of occurrence. Although not ideal, the reptile's presence had little effect on the water's usefulness. For superstitious farmers, the future success of their business relied heavily on how they chose to handle the interloper's fate.

If the snake was captured alive and allowed to go free, it was said that the land would prosper; yielding a crop that would sustain not only the farmer and his family, but everyone within their reach. This was obviously the preferred outcome for all parties involved.

If the luckless snake perished naturally while still inside the well, this signaled that a period of drought lay ahead. If the farmer, or someone acting on his behalf, took it upon themselves to kill the reptile, they would pay dearly for the deed.

As a result of taking the life of the snake, the crops on which the farmer depended in order to survive were doomed to fail. Worse still, the blight would end only when a member of the property owner's immediate family passed away. The only acceptable penance for deliberately harming a snake trapped in a well was, as it turned out, the sacrificing of another life.

We all know that roosters are a farmer's most reliable alarm clock. They rise with the sun and herald the day by throwing their heads back and letting out a series of "cock-a-doodle-doos" that would wake the dead. This is all well and good, but to have a rooster crow at midnight purportedly takes on a decidedly different meaning.

If a rooster cries out when the moon is high in the sky, the action is comparable to the sounding of a death knell for someone, or something, that dwells nearby. This ill-timed crowing is believed to signal that the life of an animal, human or otherwise, that calls the place home will come to an end within a fortnight.

For centuries, the riderless horse has been used to symbolize the loss of life suffered during times of conflict. When a fallen soldier was laid to rest, his lonesome steed would often lead the funeral procession. In the backwoods where my parents were raised, a riderless horse was not viewed as an homage to the dead, but an omen of tragedy yet to come.

If a horse showed up on someone's property with no rider in sight, rather than assuming that it had somehow escaped its enclosure, some local farmers turned to the supernatural for an explanation. An unattended, bridled equine running free was thought to be a sign that the rider was either lying injured somewhere, or that they soon would be.

If the untethered horse sported a saddle, this was thought to be a foreshadowing of dark things to come. To see a mount in this state indicated that death would soon claim the owner, most likely as a result of a riding accident, or some other occurrence involving the stray horse.

Sensing its role in future events, the animal would bolt at every opportunity in a vain attempt to stave off the inevitable. It was believed that the horse was not running away from its home, but rather from the specter of death.

Most farmers will tell you that there are certain times when it is advantageous to plant crops and others that are a recipe for disaster. One of the latter is during a full moon.

During this lunar phase, the earth is said to turn sour, causing it to reject any seeds that are laid beneath the surface. If those who tend the land remain patient for a few days, the cycle will end and the ground will become fertile once again. To plant just prior to a full moon, or in the days after it has waned, is to be assured a bountiful crop.

Chapter 2:

Birds and Insects

If a bird, most notably a sparrow, lights near a casket during a funeral, this is a sign that the dearly departed is saying a final goodbye before beginning their journey into the afterlife. If the winged visitor stays until the end of the ceremony, know that the soul it represents is taking in every face and savoring each moment until the time comes to leave the mortal world behind.

Sparrows have the distinction of being considered by some to be heavenly messengers. If you are visiting a cemetery and one of these delicate creatures lands on a nearby grave marker or monument, this suggests that a soul has dropped by to say hello.

Although there is no way of knowing if the entity being hosted by the bird is someone with whom you are familiar, or the essence of a total stranger, it doesn't really matter in the end. If you are fortunate enough to experience one of these encounters, take comfort in the knowledge that you spent time, however briefly, with a free spirit that hitched a ride on the wings of a sparrow.

Cardinals are objects of beauty, to be sure, but there is more to these feathered marvels than meets the eye. They are also thought to bring good luck and prosperity to those whose lives they grace.

The female of the species, while not as colorful as their male counterparts, are believed to be positive influences on the well-being of those they encounter. To have one of these birds visit your yard means that your future will be as brilliant as the morning sun.

To see a bright red cardinal in all his glory indicates that someone you hold dear, who is no longer living, is letting you know that they are at peace. If an individual encounters a lone cardinal on a regular basis, this is believed to mean that a deceased loved one is attempting to remain close to them for as long as possible. When this occurs, the ethereal presence should be taken for what it is: a gift from beyond.

The association between crows and the dark side is a mainstay in tales of lore. Due in part to their mysterious appearance, the presence of these highly intelligent creatures is often seen by the more superstitious among us as a sign that someone, or something, from the land of spirits is trying to open up a line of communication with the living.

It has been said that to have a single crow show up unexpectedly at a gathering means that a departed loved one, typically someone who was ostracized in life by those present, has joined the festivities. After making certain that it has been seen by all, usually by letting out a loud "caw," the uninvited guest will perch someplace nearby where it will then observe the goings-on for a while before eventually taking flight.

When a crow targets an individual rather than a group, this indicates that someone with whom the person had unfinished business has dropped by from the hereafter to remind them that all is not forgotten.

Growing up, I was told a story involving a woman and her sister who had fought bitterly over their mother's estate. One of them passed away suddenly before the matter was settled. Not long after her death, a crow began showing up at the home of the surviving sibling.

The harried woman claimed that the bird quickly became the bane of her existence, stalking her every time she left the house. It was only after she wised up and shared the proceeds from the sale of her mother's home with her deceased sister's children that the crow went along its way, never to be seen again.

To have several crows appear in an area they don't normally frequent is thought to be a warning that danger is on the horizon. It is not unusual for the ominous presence of a murder of crows to be witnessed in the days leading up to natural disasters, such as earthquakes and hurricanes.

A crow pecking on a window sill is a sign that big changes are in store for those who dwell inside. When this occurs, rather than being a harbinger of doom, this winged messenger is letting you know in advance that good fortune is headed your way.

Buzzards are scavengers that feed off the carcasses of animals that have perished either by accident or design. They also supposedly possess the ability to sense when death is approaching and will circle the area where the event will take place in anticipation of what's to come. To see a buzzard flying over a home is an indicator that someone who rests inside is not long for this world. Alerted by signals only they can sense, they operate under the mistaken assumption that they will soon feast on the meal waiting inside.

The gentle butterfly is one of nature's most magical creations. Few can resist their beauty and charm, which makes them ideal conduits to the spirit world.

To see one of these graceful creatures at a funeral signifies that the soul of the person being laid to rest, using the butterfly as its vessel, is bidding his or her final farewell before moving on to their next adventure.

If a butterfly lights on someone from out of the blue, this can be taken as a sign that a lost loved one is paying an impromptu visit. If several of Mother Nature's angels appear all at once, consider it a family reunion of sorts. This divine occurrence suggests that relatives who have passed on have gone to great lengths to spend time with those they left behind, even if only for a moment.

It is not uncommon for insects to occasionally enter homes. Normally, when they make an appearance, we shoo them out the door and get on with our lives. For those who find hidden meanings in nearly every occurrence, these unanticipated guests are often labeled as either bringers of good fortune or messengers from the afterlife, depending on the superstition being referenced.

If you discover that a lightning bug has made its way into your home, expect the unexpected. The presence of the innocuous insect indicates that a surprise is coming your way. The heralded occurrence may come in the form of a marriage or birth announcement, a long-awaited reunion, or job promotion. Whatever the case, the news will be welcomed by all.

It appears that there is no downside when one of these illuminated entities pays you a visit. Just be sure to return it to the outside world unscathed. To do otherwise won't stop the predestined event from taking place, but it will result in an unhappy ending when all is said and done.

If you happen to spy a moth fluttering around a light fixture, this suggests that a relative who has passed away has dropped by to see how you are doing. If the nocturnal visitor goes out of its way to land on a specific individual, this is taken to mean that the soul harbored by the moth is that of someone with whom that person was extremely close. Swatting the insect won't harm the departed loved one in any way, but the inhospitable act will discourage them from ever returning. On the other hand, releasing the moth into the night ensures that the gentle spirit will come again another time.

SUPERSTITIONS, OLD WIVES' TALES, & FOLKLORE 11

If you are feeling under the weather and a ladybug lands on you, the road to wellness has begun. These tiny healers, sensing that a person is ailing, will hone in on the afflicted with the sole purpose of making them whole again.

Ladybugs are also believed to spread good luck with every step. To have one walk across your arm, or other appendage, is to be blessed by the gods of serendipity.

The deathwatch beetle is a mottled insect that is most often found secreted away in old structures and other dark places where light seldom enters. These shadow dwellers measure around half an inch long and pose no harm to humans, at least not overtly.

The beetle is not dreaded for its appearance, but rather for the sounds it makes. Using its head to send out messages to others of its kind, the distinctive tapping noise that is generated by the deathwatch beetle has come to be associated with impending death, hence the name.

Apparently, once you hear the tap, tap, tap of these burrowers, your days are numbered. As legend has it, rather than communicating with its cohorts, the beetle is actually counting down how many days you have left to live.

We have all experienced the horror of discovering that a spider has invaded our safe haven. While our first instinct may be to squash the eight-legged intruder, in the world of superstitions, this impulsive act is not without consequences.

Those who take it upon themselves to end the lives of these creepy crawlers would do well to grab an umbrella before venturing out for the day. According to lore, spiders are nature's exterminators, deposited into homes from above for the sole purpose of clearing out other, more destructive, pests. To kill this creature, whose presence was carefully orchestrated by a higher power, is to break the giver's heart, resulting in a flow of tears that manifest in the form of a sudden cloudburst.

Crickets are also known to show up uninvited from time to time, although their appearance is not considered nearly as blood-curdling as that of the spider. As nature's music makers, they mean no harm, but homeowners who are a bit on the squeamish side will nevertheless swat them into oblivion. While superstition doesn't place this on the same moral level as killing a spider, it does come with a price.

Crickets, you see, are bringers of good fortune. To find one inside a dwelling is to be assured that robust health and prosperity are on the way. If this representative of positive things to come is sent packing, by whatever means, it takes the good luck that was meant for the home's occupants with it. If the cricket is killed outright, then the person whose hand did the deed can expect a spate of misfortune that will span a three-month period, which is approximately how long the insect would have lived had its life not been cut short.

The moral to these stories is a simple one: if you find that an insect or arachnid has made itself at home under your roof, rather than obliterating the tiny trespasser, let it out the way it came. After all, a selfless act of compassion benefits everyone in the end.

Chapter 3:

Man's Best Friend

Statistically speaking, black dogs are the least likely to be adopted from shelters. Much like their feline counterparts, they are stigmatized to this day by antiquated notions carried forth from the past.

One of these sentiments asserts that if you are walking outside after dark and discover that you are being followed by a black dog, you'd do well to quicken your step. Supposedly, if such a creature sets its sights on an individual during the twilight hours, this means that their soul has been marked by the ruler of the underworld. These hellhounds, as it turns out, are not dogs at all, but rather servants of the devil.

This superstition took hold centuries ago in parts of Europe when vagabonds and drunkards began disappearing in the dead of night at an alarming rate. In order to explain this frightening phenomenon, rumors began to circulate purporting that black dogs sent from the depths of Hades were roaming the streets, and outlying areas in search of vulnerable souls.

Viewed as undesirables who were obviously up to no good, the victims were often blamed for the circumstances that led to their untimely demise. As a result, the threat of mythical black dogs was used to keep wayward husbands, and those who didn't know when to say when, in line lest they fall into the clutches of Satan's soul collectors.

Most of us have encountered a stray dog at one time or another. While some of these four-legged wanderers are shy and fearful, others act as if they have known us their entire lives. It is the latter that inspired a pair of superstitions rooted in the canine's remarkable insight into the human condition.

If a dog you have never seen before runs up to you with a lolling tongue and furiously wagging tail, this is a sign that a long-lost love is thinking of you and will reenter your life in the near future. The dog, anticipating the emotions this joyous reunion will bring, cannot contain its enthusiasm.

Similarly, it is said that a stray dog who smothers a stranger with unsolicited affection is acting on the behalf of someone who has completed their transition into the afterlife. The exuberant canine is relaying to the living that a loved one for whom they still grieve has settled into their new plane of existence and is at peace.

It is believed that dogs not only possess the ability to see specters, but also have the power to drive them away if need be. Unlike most humans, canines are pure of heart, making them sworn enemies of those with ill-intentions. This includes, but is not limited to, the nastiest entities the dark realm has to offer.

While spirits seldom pose a threat to the living, they can, and do, wreak havoc if given half a chance. Dogs, sensing the presence of these supernatural interlopers, will often alert their owners that something is amiss. Unfortunately, these warnings aren't always heard or understood. When this miscommunication occurs, the family pet is tasked with taking care of the problem on their own.

Since most earthbound spirits prefer to lay low, being found out by a nosy canine is a complication they neither want or need. Realizing that they have been seen, and not wishing to be confronted at every turn, these long-suffering entities will usually retreat rather than trying to compete with the unflinching devotion of an overprotective dog.

Seeing a pitiful dog limping along on a street is a sad event in and of itself. As lore has it, to witness the animal's plight and do nothing will result in a spate of bad luck befalling the person who turned their back on a soul in need.

Fate's punishment for this neglectful act is to hobble the unfazed observer, metaphorically speaking. Much like the limping dog, the individual will soon find that the world they once knew is no more. Any success they had experienced in the past will be wiped away over time; replaced by failure at every juncture.

Divorce, financial hardship, health scares, and potential homelessness are said to await those who ignore

a dog who cannot touch all four paws to the ground. If, however, the animal is offered comfort and medical attention, the show of kindness will be rewarded tenfold.

An oft-repeated old wives' tale has it that if a dog licks a wound, yours or theirs, it will heal faster. While some canines take this to extremes, it has been shown that the action does indeed have curative properties.

The simple exercise of rubbing an injury can hasten healing since it acts to manipulate the area, sending an army of antibodies to the rescue. Unlike humans, who have notoriously dirty mouths that would put a Komodo dragon to shame, dogs' saliva contains enzymes known to hasten healing. Along with this natural antibacterial cleanser, the repetitive licking helps clear away any debris or dirt that may have gotten trapped in the wound.

So, the next time Fido wants to go to town on a bothersome scratch or bruise, don't be afraid that he or she will make things worse. On the contrary, your canine caregiver might be just what the doctor ordered.

Infertility is a painful reality for scores of hopeful parents all over the world. While medical intervention can make conception a reality, superstition tells us that couples in search of a miracle need look no further than the family dog.

It is held that if a dog lies across the belly of a woman who has tried in vain to conceive, she will learn soon afterwards that she is with child. Along those same lines, it is believed that canines can sense pregnancy in its earliest stages. If a dog suddenly begins to treat its female owner as if she is a fragile object that could break at any moment, this is taken to mean that a baby will soon be joining the family. Even though the mother-to-be may not be aware of the new life that is forming, the dog will be exceedingly gentle in order to protect not only her, but the embryo she hosts.

If a dog refuses to enter a room despite their owner's best efforts to coax them across the threshold, this suggests that something tragic has occurred in the space, or will in the near future.

The fact that dogs have an exceptional sense of smell is undeniable. It is this keen ability that is used to explain their aversion to certain rooms within a home. Capable of detecting scents that are imperceptible to humans, they often know what has transpired in a space simply by sniffing the air. As a result, if someone has died in a residence, regardless of how much time has passed since the incident occurred, a canine will pick up on this and avoid the area, not because they are afraid, but out of reverence for the deceased.

If a dog gives a wide berth to a room that has not yet been touched by death, this suggests that the Grim Reaper has set his sights on one of the occupants. Sensing that a life will be coming to an end within the confines of the room, the dog will steer clear. It would appear that the stench of death, whether realized or predicted, is something that few dogs will suffer willingly.

Some dogs seem to bay at anything and everything. For instance, we discovered soon after adopting one of our canine companions that he has an unnerving habit of howling every time he hears a siren. We eventually learned that his former owner had been taken away in an ambulance after suffering a heart attack from which he never recovered. From then on, his dog—now ours—would mimic the sound that pierced through the night as the man who had raised him from a puppy was taken away, never to return.

According to superstition, to hear a dog howling for no apparent reason means that death is approaching. Rather than merely announcing the harsh reality, the canine is actually believed to be calling it forth. Whether this is done maliciously, which is doubtful given the source, or as a merciful act is debatable. When all is said and done, as is the case with just about everything involving canines, it's best to trust their judgment. After all, they are, as anyone who shares their life with a dog will tell you, angels on earth.

Chapter 4:

The Fantastic Feline

While cats can be gentle and loving towards humans, some are not nearly as tolerant when it comes to interacting with their own species. While seeing or hearing two felines in the throes of battle is not unusual, these altercations are believed to adopt a whole new meaning when they take place in the vicinity of a funeral service.

It is said that to see cats fighting at a funeral is to bear witness to the forces of good and evil in action. In this situation, the combatants are not really cats at all, but agents of Heaven and Hell sent to vie for the soul of the dearly departed. The same holds true if cats are heard fighting outside the window of someone who is reaching the end of life's journey.

Fortunately, this only occurs in cases in which the targeted individual led a less-than-honorable existence. With their final destination up for grabs, the cat willing to go the distance determines the fate of the decedent's immortal soul.

Along those same lines, outside cats, whether they are strays or free-roaming, sometimes show up in the strangest of places; cemeteries being no exception. As superstition has it, a lone cat skulking around the headstones represents a transplanted human soul searching for a way out of its dilemma.

The discarnated essences of those who have passed on, but cannot find their way home, are fabled to dwell in graveyards, constantly on the lookout for bodies to inhabit. Since cats are thought to live their lives with two feet in this world and the other two firmly planted in the shadow realm, they make perfect hosts for lost spirits.

A cat that has taken up residence in the garden of the dead is usually given a wide berth by those who err on the side of caution. After all, a disembodied soul that has chosen a feline as its vessel is a force to be reckoned with.

It has been speculated that cats, besides being affectionate companions, are also natural-born mystics. As such, they sense things that humans either can't or won't acknowledge. It is for this reason that people who fear the dark side often keep a feline close by. A cat, in its infinite wisdom, is believed to have the capacity to not only detect the presence of evil, but also to keep it at bay by sheer force of will.

An animal's innate ability to sense danger is essential to its survival. With predators lurking around every corner, they must remain diligent or suffer the consequences. Cats are especially gifted when it comes to utilizing this sixth sense, due in part to their awareness of the vile beings that dwell in the outer reaches of our existence.

If a cat suddenly bows up and hisses at a presence only it can see, this could mean that a malevolent entity has entered the space. Realizing that it has been seen, and making no distinction between the feline protector and the humans that reside within the home, the interloper will normally opt to do its bidding elsewhere. This also holds true if a low growl emits from a cat for no apparent reason. Although the owner may observe nothing out of the ordinary, their pet knows that something is up and reacts accordingly.

With this in mind, the next time your cat exhibits behavior that makes you question its sanity, know that this was probably its intention. After all, if the performance frightened you, imagine what it did to the sinister presence that was sent packing.

It has long been thought that to have a black cat cross one's path signals danger ahead. The history of this heavily pigmented feline is filled with horrifying examples of bad luck all right; the vast majority of which fell upon the cat.

Throughout the ages, black cats have symbolized the darker nature of humanity. Often seen as a companion to witches and other fringe dwellers, they spent centuries being vilified and subjected to any number of tortures; some culminating in mass extermination of the hapless felines.

Fortunately, the black cat has also had its champions over the years whose unwavering support has allowed it to not only survive, but flourish. Fishermen who spend months at sea often take a black cat along to bring good luck to them on their treacherous journeys. It is believed among those who routinely traverse the vast oceans that if a black cat refuses to board a vessel, the mission should be aborted post haste. The animal's apprehension is taken as a sign that, if the ship leaves port, it will not be returning.

Despite the fact that some consider the black cat to be a symbol of good rather than evil, there are still those who will go out of their way to avoid crossing paths with one for fear that they will be pulled into the darkness by the mysterious feline. As is the case with many outdated ideas, superstitions die hard and centuries of being associated with misfortune are not readily forgotten.

Even though they are wonderful additions to a home, felines have an uncanny ability to get underfoot. When this happens, it often results in someone accidentally treading on the animal's tail, an action that is sometimes followed by an indignant screech or, in some cases, a retaliatory swat.

Besides the obvious repercussions, stepping on a cat's tail is said to have unforeseen consequences for the person responsible. For single women, it means that they can expect to wait a year before meeting an eligible partner. If they make a habit of the careless act, they might want to give up entirely and consider joining a convent.

In general, stepping on a cat's tail is a sure sign that bad luck will follow. Broken romances, strained finances, job loss and any number of misfortunes will supposedly plague those who offend their sensitive feline in such a manner. In order to avoid the mishap, those who notice a cat slinking near their feet would do well to watch their step. Like most things that live and breathe, even the most forgiving of felines has its limits.

Stories in which cats have allegedly predicted deaths before they occurred have made the rounds for ages. While most of these accounts were rooted in superstition, a handful of cases have come to light that are enough to give even hardcore skeptics pause.

In one well-publicized account, a nursing home in Providence, Rhode Island was the site of a series of deaths that had a peculiar common denominator: they had each occurred shortly after the patients were visited by one of the facility's resident cats, a gray and white beauty named Oscar.

Oscar, it would seem, has an amazing ability to sense when death is approaching. Rather than shying away from it, the mixed breed ball of fur is said to curl up next to the person whose time is coming to an end. After offering them comfort, he goes about his way. Within hours, the patient he visited takes their final breath.

Over a five-year period, Oscar's presence foreshadowed the deaths of fifty patients. Sadly, while it isn't unusual for nursing home residents to pass away, the fact that the cat was seen lying beside these particular patients just prior to their deaths has made a number of people wonder if he somehow knew that they were about to transition into the afterlife.

Those who are familiar with Oscar claim that he has a reputation for being somewhat of a curmudgeon, making his uncharacteristic displays of compassion all the more intriguing.

The cat's ability to sense death as it draws near is said to be so accurate that, to be on the safe side, staff members now routinely contact the families of those with whom Oscar chooses to keep company. This gives them the opportunity to spend time with their loved ones should the end result the perceptive feline is believed to foresee come to pass.

Cats are notorious for sleeping when and where they want, as anyone who has shared their home with one of these headstrong fluff balls knows all-too-well. While some are content to nestle on a sofa or in a comfy chair, others will deliberately choose to slumber in areas they know are off limits, such as the crib of an infant.

Centuries ago in parts of New England, rumors circulated that cats, working at the behest of practitioners of evil, would take the life of a newborn child if the opportunity presented itself. As a result of this concoction, when an infant was found unresponsive in its crib for no apparent reason, the family cat often took the blame. Before long, the fear of nefarious felines stealing the breath of babies became so prevalent that some parents got rid of their pets, humanely and otherwise, as a precaution.

Though it is true that some cats like to make themselves at home in cribs, it is not because they wish to harm the occupant. Felines crave warmth, so it is natural for them to be drawn to these tiny bodies that seem to exude heat from every pore. It has also been speculated that they are attracted to the aroma of milk that wafts from the mouths of sleeping infants. When a cat is seen curiously examining a baby's lips their intentions, rather than being sinister, are more likely to be an effort to find the source of the delectable smell.

Chapter 5:

Household Superstitions

In the olden days, hats were often placed on the caskets of those who were bound for the graveyard. This final act of reverence was meant to send the decedent off with their dignity firmly intact. Today, although this practice has faded with the ages, there are still those who believe that to lay a hat on a piece of furniture, especially a bed, is to call forth the Grim Reaper.

In the eyes of fate, putting a hat on a bed is tantamount to perching it atop a coffin. If this occurs, whether on purpose or by accident, a gatherer of souls will be dispatched to collect, not the owner of the hat necessarily, but the one who last slept in the bed. It is for this reason that those who are superstitious are quick to scold anyone they see carelessly tossing a hat onto a bed. They know that if it isn't removed at once, an agent of death will be summoned. Once that window of opportunity closes and the process is set in motion, there is no turning back.

Those with a more practical view of such matters will tell you that the actual reason it is considered bad luck to lay a hat on a bed is because they can carry head lice. As far as these realists are concerned, the admonishment to keep your hat off the bed is not meant to ward off grim death, but to prevent the pillow from becoming infested with these biting menaces.

Failing to remove a white tablecloth, particularly one made from cotton or linen, following a social gathering is considered an egregious act in the world of lore. While the mistake alone is enough to result in any number of minor catastrophes, to neglect the covering overnight is said to inadvertently invite death into one's home.

A white tablecloth, as opposed to any other color, is considered by providence to be a burial sheet or funeral shroud. As such, its presence alone signals that someone is in the process of departing this earth. Since all such cloths look the same to those tasked with procuring the dead, they will come looking for their mark in the hours between dusk and dawn.

Upon finding the white spread laid out with no form underneath, they take it upon themselves to wander the residence until they find a soul ripe for the taking. If this spooky tidbit isn't enough to prompt a thorough cleanup after a dinner party, I don't know what is.

Breaking a glass after making a toast is said to bring good luck to all parties involved. As this tradition goes, after drinking to good health, long life, success, happiness, and whatever else the occasion warrants, the glasses used are to be tossed against a structure such as a fireplace. The act of shattering the glass ensures that the moment is preserved for all time.

The theory behind this is that by annihilating the glasses, the words spoken prior to their destruction are sent directly to a higher power that will then see to it that the sentiments expressed in the toast come to pass.

In parts of Europe and Appalachia, it was once customary for the boots of a worker who died unexpectedly to be placed on the kitchen table to signify that their days as head of the household had come to an untimely end. Sometimes, if the person was killed in an explosion, or by some other means that resulted in the loss of their footwear, a brand new pair of shoes would be laid out as a remembrance of what used to be.

A superstition born of this bygone practice holds that to put a pair of boots or shoes on a table is to mock the dead. To commit this inadvertent act of disrespect is said to bring misfortune to all who reside in the home, whether they share in the blame or not.

Those who live and breathe by the doctrine of whispers and rumors will tell you that to bring an axe, hatchet, or any other sharpened tool that is meant to be used outdoors into an occupied dwelling is to court disaster.

If such an implement is carried into a home, thoughtlessly or on purpose, the action has doomed one, if not all, of the residents to an early death. As if that wasn't bad enough, their imminent demise will most likely come as a result of violence. This is owing to the belief that no instrument that has the power to spill blood, regardless of its intended purpose, should be allowed to cross the threshold of a space inhabited by the living. Should this occur, fate steps in to claim a soul as punishment for the careless act.

On the other hand, to leave an axe sitting upright outside the entrance to a home signals to the powers that be that the occupants are aware of the rules and are following them to the letter. This show of respect will be rewarded with fertility, thus adding members to the household instead of taking them away.

Another object meant to be used outside rather than in is the ever-resourceful umbrella. While opening one outdoors can be a lifesaver, doing so inside brings with it all sorts of negative repercussions, especially if it has never been exposed to rain. If such a thing should occur, the reversal of fortune that follows will prove devastating to the perpetrator.

From a more realistic standpoint, opening an umbrella inside a home is ill-advised since it can result in someone being gouged by the pointy tip or one of the many spokes that support the canopy. At the very least, furnishings could get damaged or broken as the umbrella unfolds in all its glory.

The admonishment that a watched pot never boils is one that is all-too-familiar. It was my mother's mantra throughout my childhood. The gist of this saying was that to place a pot on the stove and then stand watch over it until whatever was inside came to a boil was an exercise in futility. According to many a superstitious sage, my mother included, the simple act of anticipating the process prevented it from happening.

Of course, we all know that eventually the pot will boil whether we are hovering over it or not. Still, some people are taught to avert their eyes every now and then if they wish to eat in a timely fashion. Coincidentally or not, it is almost always during these brief intervals that the substance will begin to bubble away.

This superstition is not really about a pot at all. Rather, it is simply someone's clever way of saying that everything happens in its own time. To attempt to rush into something prematurely will, more often than not, end in failure. By being overeager, we sometimes impede events instead of helping them along. The takeaway is this: a pot will boil when it's good and ready; we just need to be patient.

Mirrors hold a special place in the annals of folklore and superstition. It is believed that each time they capture our reflection; they steal a portion of our essence that can never be retrieved. It is for this reason that antique mirrors are items to be avoided. Having seen decades upon decades of images, they are teeming with entities waiting to be released back into the world.

As we all know, to break a looking glass is to incur seven years of bad luck. It is also said that if a person stares into one for a lengthy period of time, their features will contort in such a way as to render them unrecognizable, even to themselves. This horrifying image is purported to be the subject's true face that is kept hidden from the world. As it turns out, these are not the most disturbing of a mirror's fabled capabilities.

It is held that to allow mirrors to face one another is to open a portal from which creatures that do not cast reflections, including the devil himself, can enter this realm. This act, once done, cannot be easily undone. In the end, the only surefire way to guard against such an occurrence is to avoid it in the first place. With this in mind, if you feel the need to have more than one mirror in a room, place them on the same wall. To do otherwise is to risk opening a gateway to and from a world inhabited by the creatures we believe exist only in our nightmares.

Although it is a habit for some people to change their bed sheets on Saturdays, this is frowned up by those in the know. Purportedly, if you change your sheets on the weekend, you will have bad dreams every night thereafter. Only when you replace them with a fresh set on a weekday will you know peace.

Changing sheets on weekends is also said to invite hardship into the home. In order to ward off this rash of bad luck, save the sheets till Monday. After all, it's better to be safe than sorry.

There are those who believe, especially in parts of Western Europe, that visitors to a home or establishment of any kind must leave by the same door from which they entered. To do otherwise, as far as they are concerned, is just asking for trouble.

By their way of thinking, the eyes of fate monitor us as we meander our way through life. The mystical guardians charged with watching our comings and goings do so without our ever being the wiser. They do not, however, babysit us every second of the day.

When we vanish through a doorway, these watchers assume that we will re-emerge from the same area at a later point. Those who decide to leave through a back door have effectively slipped through the hands of their ethereal keepers. With no one there to protect them, their downward spiral begins.

The repercussions of this innocent act are said to be swift and unforgiving. Financial ruin lies right around the corner. Relationships, however solid they may have appeared to be in the past, soon turn sour. The physical and emotional well-being of the unfortunate party begins to suffer as a result of their being left to fend for themselves in the world.

To right this wrong, the person on whom the hammer of the gods has fallen must return to the place where their troubles began and retrace their steps. On this occasion, they must enter through the door from which they previously departed.

When the time comes to say their goodbyes, it is imperative that they leave through the front entrance where their guardian awaits patiently on the other side. Since they have no sense of lost time, these agents of fate pick up where they left off and everything is, once again, as it should be.

When moving into a new residence, it is seldom a good idea to bring along unnecessary baggage. While most people know this and leave behind easily replaceable objects such as brooms and cleaning supplies, others pack up everything that isn't nailed down with the intention of using the items once they get settled. This is, as you are about to see, akin to rolling out the red carpet for bad luck.

A broom sweeps up everything in its path, including dirt tracked in on the shoes of a child, broken heirlooms, shredded love letters and any number of other things that carry with them some sort of memory. A time-worn implement introduced into a new home brings with it remnants of the past. While some are sentimental, others are best forgotten.

To use an old broom in new surroundings will not only spread past misfortunes, but also sweep away any good luck that tries to enter the area. With this in mind, if you're hoping for a fresh start, replace your antiquated cleaning tools, or risk having your dreams swept away by the stroke of a broom.

Chapter 6:

We Should Be So Lucky

Pennies, those pesky bits of currency that seem to multiply no matter how many we spend, figure prominently in the lives of the superstitious. To find one lying in a parking lot or on the street is said to spell good luck for someone, depending on which side of the coin is showing at the time.

To come upon a penny that is heads up denotes that the finder will be blessed for the next twenty-four hours. If the coin is showing tails, the person who stumbled across it must gift it to someone else, a charitable act that will bring good fortune to both parties for the remainder of the day.

If the finder of the penny opts to keep the miniscule windfall for themselves, despite the fact that it is displaying tails, the consequences will be swift and not at all pleasant. As a result of their blunder, a series of unfortunate events will befall them until midnight ushers in a new day; proving once again that it is always better to give than to receive.

It is not uncommon to hear someone remark that an individual who is in a particularly sour mood must have gotten up on the wrong side of the bed. What many don't realize is that this humorous observation can be traced back to ancient Rome where it was believed that a person's demeanor hinged almost entirely on how they chose to exit their bed.

This superstition holds that those who begin the morning by rising from the right-hand side of the mattress will be blessed with good fortune and a sense of bonhomie that will remain with them throughout the day. Those who attempt to face the world after rising from the left, however, will not only have a miserable day, but will make sure that everyone around them does the same.

This long-standing belief is thought to stem from the fact that the Latin word for left is 'sinister.' With that little tidbit in mind, it is no wonder that the ancient Romans thought it best to avoid greeting the day from that ill-fated locale.

Throughout the ages, horseshoes, arguably more than any other objects, have gained a reputation for not only bringing good luck, but also for warding off bad. To hang one above the entrance to a home with the heels pointing up is to capture blessings as they fall from the heavens.

If a horseshoe is placed with its ends facing the ground, good fortune will rain down upon everyone and everything that passes beneath the lucky charm. It seems that the horseshoe is a tireless protector, and bringer of positivity no matter which direction it is turned.

These attributes, while admirable, did not come easy. The horseshoe's gift of keeping unsavory entities at bay is fabled to be rooted in a resourceful farrier's chance meeting with a most undesirable character.

As legend has it, centuries ago, a blacksmith was approached by a loathsome creature that was neither man nor beast, walking upright on cloven feet. Cordial to a fault, even in the face of this monstrosity, the blacksmith asked if he could be of service.

The nefarious presence, which sported the horns of a ram and skin that glowed crimson, stated that it wished to be fitted with shoes. Knowing instinctively that to refuse the request would surely end badly for him, the blacksmith obliged. He did, however, have a trick or two up his sleeve.

After affixing a white-hot shoe to one of the misshapen hooves, the blacksmith nailed it in place. The beast immediately began wailing in reaction to the searing pain, despite its obvious acquaintance with fire.

It then began pleading with the blacksmith to remove the shoe, which he agreed to do, but only if the customer left and promised to never again darken the doorway of a home or establishment near which a horseshoe was displayed.

Blinded by agony, the creature readily agreed. Once the deal was brokered, the blacksmith set to work removing the shoe. The instant he was finished, the customer vanished in a puff of smoke that reeked of sulfur; never to be seen or heard from again.

And that, my friends, is how a blacksmith outsmarted the devil and gave horseshoes their unrivaled place in the world of superstitions.

Rabbits have long-been thought to possess special powers, due in part to their penchant for sheltering beneath the earth's surface for extended periods of time. Although they aren't the animal kingdom's only underground dwellers, something about this highly intelligent creature made them the center of a superstition that would be laughable were it not so gruesome.

Although its exact origins are sketchy, the practice of lopping off the foot of a bunny for good luck is thought to have its roots in ancient Celtic culture. What is known is that, long ago, someone came up with the misguided notion that because these mammals spent so much time in close proximity to the netherworld with no repercussions, their lives were somehow charmed. Even more surprising is that scores of others agreed.

Hoping that this good fortune would rub off on them, these ne'er do wells began to systematically slaughter rabbits, most often in cemeteries and churchyards. They would then remove a body part, usually the left hind foot, to keep on hand as a lucky charm. It seems that even these questionable characters weren't too keen on lugging the entire carcass around while waiting for prosperity to rain down upon them.

Whether this odd attempt at finding success has ever actually worked is doubtful, but there are still those today who carry a rabbit's foot around for good luck. Of course, if they would take time to think it through, they would realize that the severed appendage is anything but lucky. Just ask the rabbit.

Most of us, at one time or another, have found ourselves in the unenviable position of being in the middle of a conversation only to discover that the verbal well has run dry. When this happens, the awkward silence that follows can be deafening.

While trapped in the moment, the seemingly interminable quiet can be uncomfortable, to say the least. For those who think outside the box, this lull is not a bad thing at all; quite the contrary.

If two people involved in a give and take experience a sudden loss for words, this means that an angel is passing through the room. Though as mortals we don't see or hear these ethereal beings, something inside of us senses that they are close by and forces us to hold our tongues as a show of reverence.

So, the next time you fall victim to an uncomfortable pause, regardless of the circumstances, don't let it bother you. Instead of feeling uneasy, know that, if only for a moment, you were in the company of an angel.

Chapter 7:

Cemeteries & Funerals

Few places have a creep factor that can compete with that of cemeteries. This can be attributed, among other things, to the belief that the souls of those who have been laid to rest often roam the grounds after the sun goes down in an endless quest to be reunited with their earthy bodies.

While most people of sound mind avoid graveyards during the twilight hours, there are those who are drawn to these gardens of the dead like flies to honey. For the most part, since those who have passed on have little interest in associating with the living, these nocturnal interlopers have little to fear. That is, of course, unless they flaunt their gift of life in front of those who covet what they can no longer have.

It is said that to whistle when passing the gates of a cemetery is to call forth the spirits of those who rest inside. Attracted by the sound, these discombobulated souls will follow the source until he or she falls silent. If the graveyard is out of sight when this occurs, the whistler will find out soon enough that they have invited something into their life that, once it has latched on, seldom leaves of its own accord.

Similarly, those who find themselves driving or walking near a graveyard after dark are advised to hold their breath until they clear the site. If this warning is not heeded, the passerby risks inhaling a wandering spirit who will then take possession of the physical form they have been searching for which, in this case, is that of the clueless traveler.

As with most things, an ounce of prevention is worth a pound of cure. So, if you find yourself in or near a cemetery in the hours between dusk and dawn, remember to keep your lips together unless you want to bring home something other than memories.

SUPERSTITIONS, OLD WIVES' TALES, & FOLKLORE

I can remember, as a child, my mother grabbing me and pulling me away from my uncle's burial site after I inadvertently walked on the mound of earth under which he lay. Later, I received a stern lecture from, not only her, but my aunts as well. Apparently, I had placed the entire family in danger of being targeted by the unseen wraiths that they believed dwelt among the headstones.

To say that I was emotionally scarred by the experience would be an understatement. Although nothing horrible happened as a result of my having trodden on hallowed ground, the entire ordeal was upsetting to an impressionable child.

The fear of death is quite common, but the abject terror inspired by the place in which the deceased are laid to rest can be just as paralyzing for some. In an interview with talk show host Mike Douglas in the 1970s, actor George Raft illustrated how deeply some people are affected by even the mere mention of burial plots.

Raft was famous for his portrayals of gangsters and other tough guys in films of the 1930s and 40s. During his sit-down with Douglas, the interviewer asked the burly actor if anything frightened him. Raft replied that he had an irrational fear of graves. He claimed that to utter the word shook him to the very core of his being.

He wasn't kidding. George Raft, screen villain extraordinaire, had been so overwhelmed by emotion during the televised conversation that he had to dab his eyes as he spoke. As it turned out, the simple act of saying the word "grave" aloud had been enough to reduce him to tears.

There are also those who believe that if one experiences a sudden shiver, it is an indication that an animal, usually a goose, has walked over the spot where they will be interred in the future.

Whether we regard cemeteries with ambivalence or dread, the aforementioned shudder can be an unsettling reminder of what awaits each of us at the end of life's journey.

Being drenched by an unexpected downpour on the day of a graveside funeral only serves to add to the misery of those in attendance. If superstitions are to be taken seriously, there is more to this event than meets the eye. True believers will tell you that having a cloudburst interrupt this most somber of occasions is not an act of Mother Nature, but a display from the heavens.

It is held that if the sky opens up as someone is being laid to rest this means that angels are mourning a soul bound for the netherworld. So despondent are these heavenly beings by the loss of the spirit they could not save that their tears drench those gathered below.

On the other hand, if claps of thunder are heard and lightning flashes in the sky overhead, these are signs that the devil's minions are throwing tantrums in response to learning that the departing soul is bound for paradise.

Although from an emotional standpoint, no time is right for a funeral, some days are more preferable than others. This is never more evident than during All Hallows' Eve. According to lore, holding the ceremony on October 31st will result in dire consequences, not for the living, but for the person being interred.

It is rumored among those who travel in dark circles that funerals are magnets for the ghoulish entities that emerge from the underworld during Halloween. Attracted by the presence of fresh souls, they will do anything within their power to convince these easy marks to come with them. Finding themselves in a situation they had not anticipated, a spirit that is still-transitioning runs the risk of being tricked into spending eternity in the bowels of Hell.

In order to prevent this from happening, it is advised that funerals be held on days when the worst that the devil has to offer are not walking among the living. This generally means anytime other than Halloween, a twenty-four hour period during which even the purest of souls is up for grabs.

It is a long-held notion that if flowers grow naturally on a grave, the person whose name graces the marker possessed a joyful heart and clear conscience. As a reward for their innate goodness, their final resting place will be perpetually adorned with a colorful array of wildflowers; tended to lovingly by earthbound angels.

If, however, the occupant of a grave was an unsavory character who willingly brought suffering to others, the ground beneath which they sleep will be covered with an overgrowth of weeds, no matter how diligent the site's caretakers are in their efforts to keep them under control. Deemed unworthy of flowers by the forces of good, the graves of these tainted souls will display only tangles of nature's castoffs for eternity.

Singing or playing music of any kind in a graveyard is believed by some to be a means of summoning spirits. Attracted to the sound, these disembodied entities will converge and follow the source until it falls silent. While this is not necessarily a bad thing in and of itself, the unintentional interaction can lead to trouble if those involved are not careful.

Since there is no way of knowing if the otherworldly beings that are reputed to lurk in cemeteries are harmless or parasitic in nature, it's best to keep singing to a minimum while in their domain. In the frighteningly accurate words of 18th century French poet Remy de Gourmont, "Demons are like obedient dogs, they come when they are called."

If you happen to be in a cemetery, as a visitor of course, and notice that the earth atop a particular grave appears to be more worn down than that of its neighbors, this marks the occupant as a leader of spirits.

As the story goes, a burial site on which the grass seems to be perpetually trampled, so much so that the dirt underneath is revealed, marks the spot as one frequented by nonliving beings that congregate in the afterhours.

While most souls do not choose to inhabit cemeteries, those that do often find themselves lost in the unfamiliar surroundings. As a result, they are constantly searching for guidance. If they find the resting place of someone who was in charge of others during their lifetime, such as a leader of men or a mother of a large brood, they gravitate towards that person's grave in hopes of finding solace.

So, if you ever come upon a grave that looks as if it has seen more than its fair share of visitors, consider the possibility that the person whose remains are interred in the spot is acting as a mentor for the dead who are unable to move on.

Planting a rose bush on someone's final resting place will not only serve to beautify the site, but just might save the immortal soul of whoever lies beneath the earth. Roses, a symbol of love, are intolerable to the vile beings that stalk cemeteries in search of lost spirits. The presence of roses will deter any demonic forces that happen to be lurking nearby. Not only that, but they will also attract angelic guardians who will watch over the soul of whoever lies in the plot until the time comes to guide them home.

SUPERSTITIONS, OLD WIVES' TALES, & FOLKLORE 39

Attending a funeral service is never a pleasant experience. The crushing sense of grief is often palpable, whether the ceremony is held indoors or at the gravesite of the deceased. As superstition has it, opportunistic specters, attracted by the overwhelming sorrow that hangs in the air, have a tendency to latch onto unsuspecting mourners. Once they have honed in on a target, these parasites will follow them wherever they go, determined to do anything to resume their place among the living.

In order to prevent this from happening, those who visit graveyards for any reason are advised to make several stops before heading home. Since these vagabond spirits are thought to have lost all sense of direction, they become easily disoriented which allows the unwitting host to lose them in a crowd.

This is one reason that people tend to gather in restaurants following memorial services, whether they are aware of this longstanding superstition or not. While it is true that misery loves company, it is equally true that there is safety in numbers. If things go according to plan, the displaced soul, finding itself adrift in a sea of unfamiliar faces, will realize that it is woefully out of place and wander off to parts unknown.

If a clueless mourner opts to forgo tradition and head straight home, well, we've all seen enough horror movies to know that it won't be long before they find their life turned upside down by a destructive, if unseen, presence. By the time the host catches on to what is happening their fate has been sealed.

To suddenly be aware that someone is following close on your heels is enough to make anyone's heart skip a beat. When this occurs within the confines of a cemetery, the apprehension is taken to the next level.

If you hear footsteps behind you while walking in a graveyard, despite there being no one else present, you would do well to leave the grounds on the double. Finding that you are being trailed in a cemetery can be an indicator that you have been targeted by an opportunistic spirit. Should this occur, keep walking and, whatever you do, don't turn around. If the entity sees your face, it will retain the image from that day forward. From then on, no matter where you go, your unearthly shadow will follow. Unfortunately, whether you see them or not, you have invited a dark force into your life and it is there that they will stay.

Chapter 8:

Pregnancy and Motherhood

While pregnancy brings with it great joy, it does not protect the expectant mother from outside sorrows. If someone close to her passes and she is asked to attend their funeral, a superstitious mother-to-be knows to respectfully decline. If she chooses to tempt fate and show up at the service, she runs the risk of having the soul of her unborn child switched with that of an unscrupulous spirit.

According to this piece of lore, unbeknownst to the living, displaced souls perpetually wander graveyards searching for a way back into the world they once knew. While it is nearly impossible to secure an adult form, the developing body of a child in utero is considered a perfect vehicle for a restless entity's rebirth.

Upon sensing the pregnant woman's presence, opportunistic spirits will vie for the soul of the fetus. The one that emerges triumphant will take the baby's place, the mother never the wiser. From that day forward, she will carry and eventually give birth to the changeling.

This scenario, while implausible, is so disturbing that those familiar with the superstition will often warn expectant mothers to steer clear of cemeteries until after they give birth.

There is a laundry list of admonishments regarding scissors, among them the ever-popular don't run while holding the implement in your hand, lest you fall and be impaled. For expectant mothers, however, the implications are a bit more ominous.

Those wise to the ways of lore know to keep scissors, and other sharp objects, far away from pregnant women. To have these tools lying around is believed to play into the hands of unseen demons who wish nothing more than to sever the umbilical cord prematurely, resulting in miscarriage or stillbirth.

Exhaling too forcefully is a belief that a handful of my overcautious relatives used to tout, especially during birthday celebrations. If one or more of the attendees happened to be expecting, they were asked to refrain from helping inflate balloons or blow out candles, even if they were the guest of honor.

These precautions were not meant to put a damper on the festivities, but rather to protect the unborn fetus. The theory behind this was that if a pregnant woman exhaled too forcefully, she might inadvertently expel the baby's soul. If this occurred, the much-anticipated child, now an empty shell, would be lost forever.

Another superstition that was batted about in my family centered round the consequences a sudden scare would have on a pregnancy, especially if it involved insects.

As if to illustrate that this notion was true, my aunt was startled by a praying mantis one day while tending to her garden. Several months pregnant at the time, she immediately took to the house, overcome by the fear that the mental trauma she experienced would somehow impact the baby she was carrying.

To her relief, she ended up giving birth to a healthy baby boy. That would have been the end of the story had it not been for the way he came out of the womb. According to family gossip, which was repeated endlessly over the years, he was born with his arms crossed in front of him and his hands pointed downward, mimicking the pose of a praying mantis.

As bizarre as it sounds, those present at the time swore that the account was accurate. From then on, they doubled down on their assertion that if an expectant mother experiences a sudden fright her baby will not only retain memories of the harrowing event, but relive it as they enter the world.

Let's be honest, while all babies are adorable in their own way, not many are painfully beautiful. Of course, that doesn't stop some people from exclaiming that every cherub they lay eyes on is the most gorgeous thing they've ever seen. As superstition has it, their well-meaning exaggeration could end up doing more harm than good.

If one truly wants to do the newborn a favor, rather than extolling their beauty for all to hear, they should downplay it by announcing that they've seen cuter. As cruel as this may sound, the intention is not to insult the infant or its parents, but to keep the devil at bay.

You see, it is thought that the minions of the netherworld are always on the lookout for babies to whisk away to their fiery domain. These evil entities are, however, quite finicky and will only steal the most perfect of human specimens. By declaring loud and clear that the baby in question is ugly, for lack of a better word, the crass observer is only looking out for the child's immortal soul.

With this in mind, if you ever come across someone who either keeps their lips together when asked to judge a baby's looks or blurts out something less than complimentary, don't take offense. They are simply trying to stay one step ahead of the devil, or so we hope.

It isn't unusual for a baby to come into the world sporting a birthmark. Normally, these tiny imperfections are harmless and serve only to enhance the uniqueness of this bundle of joy. How they got there in the first place is, as you will see, where superstition enters the room.

Some believe that birthmarks develop when a mom-to-be denies herself a food or beverage that she craves. For instance, marks resembling wine stains that appear on a baby's skin are said to be the result of the mother's having ignored her body's desire for a glass of port.

Others speculate that birthmarks mirror injuries sustained by the mother during the latter part of her pregnancy. An example of this would be if a woman happened to bump into something hard enough to leave a bruise or abrasion while in her third trimester. As if to empathize with its mother, the baby will be born sporting a discoloration in the same size and shape as her contusion.

To round things out, there are those who believe that birthmarks are a gift from the heavens. A friend's daughter, for instance, was born with a pigmented patch of skin that they referred to as "God's thumbprint" for its uncanny resemblance to the appendage. Since no one has ever pinpointed the exact cause of birthmarks, nothing is out of the realm of possibility.

As far as most people are concerned, cracks in the pavement are nothing to be alarmed about. For those schooled in the teachings of superstition, these innocuous-looking fissures are thought to be passageways to other dimensions.

Somewhere along the line, the fear of what lies beneath these openings led to the oft-repeated rhyme: "Step on a crack, break your mother's back." The philosophy behind this threatening bit of prose was that to tread upon one of these fractures was to awaken the evil entities that reside just below the surface.

Should this occur, it was said that these volatile beings would exact their revenge, not on the perpetrator, but on the one they deemed responsible for that person's existence. The subsequent break in the back of the unwitting mother was said to emulate the crack that their offspring thoughtlessly violated.

The moral of this story is, apparently, to be mindful of your surroundings. After all, one misstep can have dire consequences, not only for you, but for those you hold most dear.

Chapter 9:

Venturing Into the Dark Side

There are ghost stories galore that revolve around everyday people who claim to have been stalked by featureless forms that appeared from out of nowhere, seemingly overnight. When these events occur, it is often assumed that these entities are somehow connected to a haunted dwelling or cursed object.

In folklore, it is put forth that these mysterious figures are actually on a mission from the underworld. In some instances, it is believed that these specters are not displaced souls at all, but phantom collectors sent from beyond to settle debts that were left unpaid in previous incarnations.

Past-life creditors, as they are known, are unleashed on those who died owing money to someone who took their vindictiveness to the grave. Upon reaching the shadow realm, these unforgiving souls call upon the devil's henchmen to even the score.

By the time the collectors come calling, the defaulter is living life anew; completely unaware of the debts they accrued in their past lives. It is only when these apparitions are seen lurking in the shadows, or show up in the background of photographs, that the clueless mark realizes that they have been targeted by something decidedly sinister. Knowing that they are in trouble, but powerless in the face of pure evil, the victim's life begins to spiral out of control.

Since money is of no value to the dead, vengeance is exacted as the collector's see fit. It is claimed that at the onset of the visitations, the person at the center will fall ill. The ailment could be mild or quite serious, depending on the level of debt that remained on the books.

After days, weeks, or even months of harassment, the otherworldly avengers will depart, satisfied that the debtor has learned their lesson. The reprieve is, however, only temporary. The score will only truly be settled when the unforgiven party reaches the land of the dead where the ultimate punishment awaits.

The assertion that blood possesses special powers has been promoted in the occult, as well as in some factions of Christianity, for centuries. This belief stems from the notion that blood, but only that which is freshly spilt, holds powers that can be used for both good and evil. That being said, only the most depraved among us actually attempt to put this concept to the test.

It is important to note that the blood in question cannot have been spilled by the person wishing to use it for their own devices. Rather, the event that resulted in the mishap must occur organically. An individual looking to procure this precious liquid can only do so if they stumble upon it completely by accident, under any other circumstances, it is rendered useless.

For those who believe is such things, it has been put forth that if one witnesses an accident in which injuries have occurred, they need only dip a piece of cloth into the blood of the unfortunate victim, living or otherwise, in order to harness its magic.

After pilfering the life-sustaining substance, the keeper of the cloth can use it to wish for good fortune, or alternatively, to lay a curse upon someone they believe has done them irreparable harm. Of course, as with most things, this act of vengeance is not without consequences.

If the person uses that which they have obtained to the detriment of another, they will pay for this at a later date by having their own blood spilled in a similar fashion and, more often than not, used for dishonorable purposes. The process then becomes a perpetual circle that is broken only when the blood is left untouched until it is allowed to dry, at which time it loses all potency. When this occurs, the curse is ended and the dark pall lifted.

While most of us give little thought to the color of ink with which we sign our name, in some parts of the world, this seemingly insignificant detail could mean the difference between life and death.

In South Korea, a longstanding belief purports that if a person writes their signature in red, they might as well be signing their death warrant. Since the names of those who have passed on are traditionally recorded in crimson, to write the name of someone who lives and breathes in a hue reserved for the dead is to infer that they are equals in the eyes of fate. Consequently, this act born of ignorance announces to the gods that the careless party's soul is ready to be claimed.

If someone with whom you are acquainted takes it upon themselves to write your name in red, you would do well to view them with caution. Their intentions, if this superstition holds true, may be somewhat less than pure.

It is common knowledge that performing acts of personal grooming outside the privacy of our homes is distasteful. Besides being unsanitary, not many people wish to observe a stranger trimming their fingernails, or flossing their teeth in public. Even so, there are those who have no qualms about giving the world a peek into their somewhat offensive routines.

The superstition attached to this practice isn't concerned with the hygienic issues that could arise from such actions, but rather the practical ones. It is believed that to leave parts of your physical form lying around, such as discarded fingernail clippings or stray hairs, is to open yourself up to more trouble than you can handle.

Someone with a score to settle, or even a total stranger who possesses both a cruel streak and a passing knowledge of black magic, can use these cast-offs to curse unsuspecting marks. Once they have a piece of their target in hand, they gain access to the inner workings of that person's mind and body. With this powerful tool at their disposal, there's no end to the harm they can do.

The lesson to be gleaned from this bit of lore is fairly obvious: unless it is your goal to give an enemy, known or unknown, a gift that can be used against you, either do your grooming in private or clean up after yourself. Any other option could end badly for you, in more ways than one.

Surely, there can be nothing wrong, even in the nitpicky universe of superstitions, with enjoying a stick of sugary sweet gum whenever the notion strikes you. There isn't, of course, unless you decide to indulge after the sun goes down. As is the case with most things that take place in the darkness, to chew gum in the twilight hours has a hidden meaning, and it's not at all pleasant.

If one chooses to chew gum during the day, the worst they can expect is eventual tooth decay. After dark, however, it is believed that the gooey gob of goodness takes on the properties of something not nearly as appealing.

According to Turkish superstition, to chew the sticky substance after sundown, especially during special occasions, is akin to gnawing on human flesh. You read that right. Believe it or not, there are those who firmly believe that this innocent act transforms the gum chewer into an unwitting cannibal. It's gruesome and makes little sense, but there it is.

To be on the safe side, if you ever find yourself in Turkey and are invited to an after-hours shindig, stick with mints. To do otherwise, if this nasty piece of lore holds true, can turn even the most mild-mannered individual into a flesh eater.

Chain letters, those unsolicited correspondence that promise good fortune to those who pass the message along to others, and bad luck to those who don't, have been making the rounds for as long as anyone can remember. In today's digital age, purveyors of these writings are able to reach more people than ever before, leaving those who are superstitious by nature with no choice other than to do as the letter directs or face the consequences.

Traditionally, chain letters prey on the recipient's fear of the unknown. In some instances, the gist of the communication is benign, promising spiritual rewards to those who send a specific number of copies to their friends and family. In other, less ethical instances, the original sender uses scare tactics in order to prevent the chain from being broken.

Some unscrupulous senders warn those they are attempting to dupe that harm will come to their loved ones unless they follow the letter's instructions to the T. Even those who don't put stock in such nonsense will often give in and fire off ten or twelve copies to their unsuspecting circle of acquaintances rather than tempt fate.

People who send chain letters in hopes of financial gain will usually ask that money be included in the transaction. Back in the day, a person who received such a letter was advised to attach a dime to the duplicates before posting them. If everyone followed through with the request, the originator ended up with a tidy sum when the chain eventually came full-circle.

Oftentimes, these letters include anecdotes of what happened to non-believers who tossed out or deleted the correspondence. These stories gleefully share details of the horrid luck that laid waste to these misguided souls prior to their lives ending tragically, often at the hands of an anonymous punisher. These cautionary tales remind those hesitant to participate in such folly that the individuals they referenced would still be alive and well, if only they had taken the time to forward the letters.

SUPERSTITIONS, OLD WIVES' TALES, & FOLKLORE 51

Most of us know that chain letters are simply words on a sheet of paper or computer screen that possess no special powers. As such, their content should be taken with a grain of salt. Still, there are those who believe that their lives, and those of the people around them, hinge on perpetuating the chain. And, so the phenomenon continues, as it has for centuries.

Children know better than most that allowing your hands or feet to dangle over the edge of a mattress is equivalent to ringing the dinner bell for the monster that resides under the bed. The terrifying notion that nocturnal predators are just waiting for the opportunity to pounce on an appendage that escapes the safety of the covers is so ingrained in some people that it stays with them well into adulthood.

If a heavy sleeper lets their guard down and the unthinkable happens, well, no one knows for certain what comes next since the hungry dead seldom leave scraps. Although the origins of this superstition are unknown, it is believed that it probably stemmed from the attempts of harried parents to keep their young ones tucked in at night.

The number thirteen has long been considered unlucky. The idea is so ingrained in society that buildings seldom have thirteenth floors. It is also why Friday the 13th is thought to be a day when the veil that normally protects us from the eyes of evil is at its thinnest point. It is during this twenty-four hour period that we are believed to be at our most vulnerable.

The origins of the number thirteen's questionable reputation are a bit sketchy. One theory is that it stems from a Norse legend in which twelve gods were invited to attend a dinner party. During the festivities, a thirteenth guest, the god Loki, showed up unexpectedly. Upon seeing his cohorts enjoying themselves without him, a confrontation ensued during which another god, Balder, was murdered. At the moment of his death, the mortal world was said to have been plunged into total darkness. It is thought that the chaos that resulted from the thirteenth guest's vengeful act left the number forever tainted.

Thirteen is seen by some as a bringer of bad luck due to its association with the crucifixion of Christ. This stems from the belief that thirteen apostles were present at The Last Supper. Christ was killed on the following day, which happened to be a Friday.

During any given year, the thirteenth falls on a Friday at least once. If January 1st is on a Sunday, then the unlucky date will appear three times on the calendar. When the day rolls around, those who believe that Friday the 13th and bad luck are synonymous often choose to interact as little as possible with the outside world until the clock strikes twelve and things return to normal. That is, until next time.

Common sense tells us that walking backwards is seldom a good idea. After all, if we can't see where we're going, any number of mishaps can occur. In the realm of folklore, however, this careless act can result in something far worse than a simple fall.

Since walking backwards is unnatural for humans, to do so is believed to attract the attention of evil spirits who may be hovering between worlds. Sometimes, as in this instance, standing out from the crowd piques the interest of these lecherous entities who will then cross over from the dark side.

So out of the ordinary is the action of walking backwards that it is even rumored to capture the eye of the devil himself. Unfortunately, once he has set his sights on someone, there is no way to reverse the process, so to speak.

The person who for whatever reason decided to go against the grain, soon finds that they have inadvertently invited the devil to accompany them home. As a result, the life they once knew comes to an abrupt end, replaced by misfortune, ill-health, and eventual madness.

This horrifying outcome can be easily avoided by simply facing forward when walking, making what lies ahead clearly visible. When one can see where they're going, they are less likely to stumble, both physically and spiritually speaking.

It's been said that every person walking the earth has a twin that they are unaware of somewhere in the world. If we are lucky, we live our lives without ever encountering this mirror image of ourselves. Not everyone, however, is so fortunate.

Tales of these mysterious twins, known as doppelgangers, have been around since the 17th century. The word, which literally means "double-goer" in German, is defined as "a ghostly counterpart of a living person." The school of thought behind this phenomenon is that the duplicate is not another individual at all, but instead is their essence that has somehow managed to transcend the body and wander around independently.

To encounter one's doppelganger is believed to signal that death is forthcoming. In 1860, a man who would change history was said to have cast his eyes upon his astral twin, an unintentional act that would seal his fate.

On the night he was first elected President of the United States, Abraham Lincoln decided to rest for a while on the settee in his bedroom. While lying down, he happened to catch a glimpse of his reflection in a floor-length mirror that was situated across the room. He knew instantly upon viewing the image that something was terribly wrong.

Getting up for a closer look, he saw that, although his body appeared normal, two distinct faces were reflected in the glass. One was an accurate depiction while the other was ghostly pale and devoid of life. As he stared in disbelief, the frightening image faded from view. A few days later, the scenario repeated itself.

Intrigued by what he had seen, Lincoln related the story to his wife, Mary Todd. Familiar with the ominous nature of the doppelganger, she told her husband that she feared the deathly image was a sign that he would be elected to a second term, but would not live to see it through.

For the next five years, until the evening of his assassination, Lincoln lived with the knowledge that his days were numbered. He had been warned in advance by his own reflection.

Before getting into the details of the following macabre belief, be forewarned that it is not for the faint of heart. If you are at all squeamish, feel free to skip to the next chapter.

In the days before embalming became a common practice, it wasn't unusual for bodies to moan, groan, shift, or otherwise act out while awaiting burial. Even though these functions were perfectly normal aspects of decomposition, superstitions soon arose to explain the actions being performed by the physical forms of the recently deceased.

When an expectant mother died before giving birth, it was considered to be one of the worst tragedies that could befall a family, and rightly so. On rare occasions, however, things didn't end there. To the horror of those tasked with preparing the body for burial, depending on how far along the woman was in her pregnancy at the time of death, biology would sometimes take over.

As the process of decomposition set in, gases would build up in the mother's body, causing her to expel the fetus. This process is known in the medical community as postmortem fetal extrusion. Those of the superstitious ilk viewed it as something a bit more metaphysical.

They believed that a woman who passed with an unborn baby inside her would be denied entry into Heaven. Unable to move forward or back, she would remain in limbo, never seeing or holding the infant she was doomed to carry for eternity. The explanation for this was that there was no place set aside in the afterlife for a single entity that harbored two souls.

Well-aware of this, it was said that a woman who delivered a fetus postmortem, whether it be on her deathbed, in the mortuary, or even in the confines of her coffin, had done so in order to free both her soul and that of her child. Rather than being a physiological occurrence, this event was seen as a mother's desperate attempt to ensure that she and the life she helped create would be reunited in the hereafter.

While coffin births, as they are commonly known, are rare, they still occur to this day. Disturbing in every way, this is one superstition that is rooted in real events, gruesome though they may be.

Chapter 10:

An Odd Hodgepodge of Beliefs

Lore involving the deeper meaning to the phenomenon of an ever-fading photograph is popular in the area of West Virginia where my parents grew up. It is rooted in the notion that an image captured forever, whether it is on film or canvas, retains the essence of whoever is depicted in the piece. From that point on, the progression of their life is reflected in the portrait.

It is believed that as the picture fades, so too does the life it portrays. This unsettling process continues even after death. While looking through old photo albums, if a picture is discovered in which the subject's features are no longer discernible, it is assumed that they have been deceased for a good length of time. If the image is only slightly faded, they have barely settled in the grave. If the photo is so far gone that the person cannot be identified by sight alone, this means that they have ceased to have any connection to the mortal world.

While few people purposely drop money on the ground, it isn't unusual for change to fall from a pocket or purse by accident. When this happens, the person responsible normally picks up what has been lost and the incident is forgotten; providing, of course, that they are not particularly superstitious.

When coins hit a floor, or other hard surface, the sound is said to awaken the imps that dwell in the world that lies parallel to our own. Alerted by the clinking of change, these greedy hobgoblins will stop at nothing to take possession of what they presume to be gold. It would seem that the precious metal is a coveted commodity in both the inner and outer reaches of existence.

SUPERSTITIONS, OLD WIVES' TALES, & FOLKLORE

If the one who dropped the money picks it up immediately and secrets it away, the interlopers will return to where they came from, penniless and dejected. If, however, the coins are left in place, they will be collected by the imps who will then proceed to attach themselves to the source in hopes of garnering another windfall. Though careful to stay out of sight, they will make their presence known by causing minor accidents that result in more money being spilled.

While the party who can't seem to keep track of their loose change tries to make sense of their frustrating bouts of clumsiness, the opportunistic sprites fill their pockets with coins until their avarice is sated.

To have one foot in the grave normally means to be nearing the end of one's days due to illness or old age. While it did so in my family as well, it also had another connotation that was a bit more disturbing.

It isn't unheard of to be walking through a field, or even on your own lawn, and inadvertently step in a hole that has been strategically placed by a burrowing animal of some sort. When this occurs, a twisted ankle, often accompanied by a bruised ego, is usually the worst that can happen.

In some circles, including my own, such an act instantly subtracts a year from your life expectancy. The twisted logic at the center of this belief is that when your foot has been underground for any reason, you have unintentionally hastened the process of death. As far as fate is concerned, it would seem that a foot in the earth moves you one step closer to a foot in the grave.

A popular old wives' tale holds that waking a sleepwalker, rather than snapping them out of their stupor, will actually scare them to death.

While this belief makes a modicum of sense, there appears to be no truth to it.

While the shock of finding themselves roaming the house when they should be tucked into bed may irritate the nocturnal wanderer, it will not induce a heart attack or any other life-threatening reaction. Even so, it is advised that sleepwalkers be quietly directed to a safe place where, hopefully, they can slumber in peace.

The curse of withered flowers is one that was popular with several members of my extended family. The subject usually came up when flowers that were growing in the yard, or on rare occasions, those purchased from a shop, began to wilt prematurely.

While most people would take this as an indication that the flowers had fallen victim to some form of blight, my relatives instantly jumped to the conclusion that a bad soul was nearby. According to them, trees, flowers, and even grass could sense the presence of evil and withered in its wake.

Although the malevolent force that had caused the flowers to shed their petals and die was never identified, the thought was spooky enough to keep us jumping at our own shadows for days to come. It was only when healthy flowers began to bloom that it was assumed that the storm had passed.

To give a clock as a gift is, according to folklore, one of the most egregious acts a person can commit. While the giver may have only the best of intentions, the introduction of a timekeeper into a house by someone who does not live there supposedly begins the countdown to the homeowner's death.

Clocks herald not only the moment of our birth, but also the hour of our death. This is something we all know and, for the most part, never give much thought. If, however, the device that will someday mark the end of our life is given to us by a third party, they have unintentionally sped up the inevitable in the eyes of fate. From that point on, each tick of the clock is an hour lost for the one who holds deed to the property. The process, once set in motion, will continue until the clock is removed from the premises, or its rightful owner takes their final breath, whichever comes first.

Yellow, while bright and sunny, is one color not to be toyed with. So risky is this hue that to give a gift of yellow is to doom the recipient to an early grave. Likewise, it is held that if you are given something yellow, you'd better enjoy it while you can for it will be the last gift you will ever receive.

The bad connotation associated with yellow is thought to stem from both its prevalence in the design of funeral wreaths and its place in the realm of black magic. It doesn't help that it is, allegedly, the devil's favorite color.

For commercial fishermen, yellow is a no-no aboard their vessels. Bananas are normally forbidden, not only for their hue but also for their reputation for harboring parasites. Yellow objects of any kind, when brought onto a boat, will threaten not only the catch, but the safety of the captain and crew.

In folklore, to see blood on the Moon is a sure sign that someone close to you will come to harm within three days. The prophesized event may be as minor as a scraped knee or so serious that it will bring the chosen one to the brink of death. Since fate's overseers are loath to divulge their secrets, in the end, it becomes a game of wait and see.

A crimson moon is a natural phenomenon that occurs every two and a half years or so during a lunar eclipse. When this happens, the

Moon, which is always full at the time, takes on a reddish hue as the Earth passes between it and the Sun. While this occurrence may be considered run-of-the-mill by some, those who live their lives by the laws of superstition view it as an omen. For them, the blood that is spilled on the Moon is a grim warning of things to come.

If we stop and think about it, bells play important roles in our lives from early childhood. They do, after all, direct us through the school day, informing us when class begins and ends. In fact, there are few sounds more pleasurable to a child's ears than the final bell each year that announces that summer has at last arrived.

Bells symbolize beginnings and endings, but they are also tools used to signal impending danger; hence the term "warning bell." In lore, these instruments are believed to not only call upon the forces of light, but also to repel the purveyors of evil.

Demons are believed to have a paralyzing fear of loud noises. The ringing of bells is, for them, an intolerable assault they will not suffer willingly. Realizing this, church founders began installing chapel bells on houses of worship, the pealing of which sent the message to those with ill-intentions that they were not welcome on the grounds.

Wind chimes, while similar to bells, are thought to be even more effective at keeping bad energy at arm's length. What's more, their hypnotic music, powered by the air around them, also has the ability to attract benevolent spirits whose only purpose is to keep watch over the living.

Hanging a set of wind chimes outside of a dwelling will supposedly ward off nefarious beings bent on causing upheaval in the lives of the occupants. The tinkling sound that grows louder with every shift in the breeze is so unbearable for these outliers that they will retreat rather than be exposed to the maddening crescendo.

Those wishing to monitor spirit activity occurring right under their nose can do so by placing wind chimes inside their residence. With no source of wind within the walls, any unexplained movement is thought to indicate that a spirit is present. The soft tinkling of the tubular bells is their way of letting those who occupy the space know that all is well; the forces of good are on the job.

If wind chimes that are hung indoors begin to move wildly, this means that an unwanted presence has entered the scene. Sensing this, the protective spirits will whip the instrument into action, driving the malevolent intruder out before it can take hold of the souls of those who shelter inside.

Monobrows, also known as unibrows, occur when a person's eyebrows form an unbroken line across their forehead. While some who sport this unique feature wear it proudly, others choose to shave or wax the hair growing above their nose to keep stares to a minimum. In folklore, eyebrows with no separation have meanings ranging from the sublime to the ridiculous.

Some claim that those with prominent monobrows possess above average intelligence. By their estimation, the individual's mind is so fertile that it encourages hair growth across the forehead. This overgrowth is thought to mimic the constant hub taking place beneath the surface.

Along those same lines, a man who chooses to show off his monobrow is viewed as, not only an intimidating figure, but also virile to the extreme. Considered the ultimate man's man, their company is said to be coveted by women who long for a large family. While not everyone's cup of tea, a bushy monobrow suggests that the one boasting the unusual feature will have no trouble fathering multiple children.

In the days when monstrous predators were thought to stalk the moors, those with monobrows were forced to keep their ever-growing hair under control or risk being branded a werewolf. Upon seeing facial hair growing where it was not meant to be, paranoid villagers assumed that things were not what they seemed. Unable to hide their true nature, even in the light of day, the subject of their suspicions was forced to assimilate, or face the wrath of those around them.

Fresh-cut flowers are a lovely addition to any home. Dried flowers, on the other hand, are an entirely different matter. In the world of superstitions, flowers that no longer show any sign of the vibrancy they once flaunted are seen as death personified. Consequently, to display these dried remnants for all to see is said to bring not only bad luck into a residence, but also the interminable stench of decay. Once a house is marked as being a place in which death is welcome, it won't be long before collectors sent from the hereafter will be making an appearance.

One would think that, even among the devoutly superstitious, there could be no consequences to wishing someone a happy birthday. That assumption is correct, provided that the exclamation is not made prior to the big event.

Apparently, offering congratulations to someone before their actual birthday is frowned upon, unless your intention is to ruin their life. Even if your heart is in the right place, the innocent gesture is said to have lasting repercussions for the person to whom the proclamation was directed.

By heralding the event before it occurs, the well-wisher has doomed the subject to a year of bad luck. In extreme cases, such as instances in which a party is thrown in advance, the honoree may not live to see the actual anniversary of their birth. Judging from this, it would appear that those in charge of our eternal clocks are not only sticklers for exact dates, but also mercilessly unforgiving.

Calling someone by the wrong name can be embarrassing under the best of circumstances. This bit of kismet maintains that if you mistakenly address someone, the person whose name escaped your lips by accident is thinking about you at that very moment.

This is said to occur when the people involved are exceedingly close, such as a pair who are blood-related or have shared intimacy on some level. So strong is their mutual bond that, when one focuses their thoughts on the other, that person is so overwhelmed by the flood of emotions that suddenly wash over them that they can't help but blurt out the name of their kindred spirit.

While this is heartwarming in a way, it can also be troublesome if the relationship between the parties involved is clandestine. Sometimes, as in this instance, serendipity can be quite the blabbermouth.

Lights that appear from out of nowhere, such as orbs, glowing mists, or streaks in the night sky are thought by some spiritualists to represent the souls of those who have passed on, but remain attached to this world. Unable to manifest in physical form, these ethereal wanderers appear to the living as various forms of light.

Unexplained illuminations are also known to signal that someone has passed from this earth. On a spring night in 1964, at around three o'clock in the morning, my father and uncle were driving on a country road on their way home from a fishing trip. As they made their way down the mountain, their progress was halted by a blinding light that enveloped both their truck and the woods around them. Although it lasted for only a few seconds, the intense rays were something they could neither explain nor forget.

The following day, my parents learned that my maternal grandfather had died from a massive stroke at 3am. Although these events took place before I was born, the story was related countless times over the years by family members who were convinced that the mysterious light was my grandfather's way of saying goodbye.

Chapter 11:

Witches in Lore

We have all seen the images, in books and on film, of witches gathered around a steaming metal pot, stirring away at the ghastly concoction that is brewing inside as they cackle maniacally. If this ever actually occurred, it probably had more to do with a hearty stew than black magic, but that didn't stop the spread of rumors to the contrary.

Ancient Celts believed that witch's cauldrons contained souls that had been sent from Hell to await reincarnation. At the request of their lord and master, witches were tasked with keeping these abhorrent spirits viable by agitating them until the time came for them to be returned to the world of the living.

Another slightly less disturbing explanation was that the oversized pots held the ingredients necessary to create potions that would later be used for either good or evil, depending upon the circumstances. These fixings could consist of benign offerings such as herbs foraged from nearby forests, or distasteful fare like the innards of woodland creatures that were sacrificed for the sake of the spell that was being fashioned.

When all was said and done, whatever was brewing, be it souls, spells, or a tasty vegetable soup, the bubbling cauldron became synonymous with the witch and vice versa.

In the olden days, a female who wore gloves and refused to remove them when asked was viewed as having something to hide. During the periods in which people feared that witches lurked around every corner, a woman's reluctance to show her hands in public could be a death sentence.

This notion stems from the belief that, instead of traditional fingernails, witches sported claws. Since exposing these features to the world would give away their true identity, they were forced to keep their hands covered at all times lest their secret be revealed.

Besides fingernails, it was also put forth that witches lacked ten very important appendages, namely, their toes. Since this made walking exceedingly difficult, they were gifted shoes with turned up points by their creator that allowed them to get around without exposing their anomaly to the unforgiving masses.

On top of being born without fingernails and toes, witches were also supposedly unable to grow hair on any part of their body. If this was truly the case, it would explain their fondness for wide-brimmed hats which, while not flattering, helped to keep the wigs they were forced to wear secured to their heads.

The absence of eyebrows was easily taken care of by using a steady hand and a piece of charcoal to simulate the real thing. Fortunately for them, drawn-on brows were popular then just as they are now. In this case at least, it would appear that even the much-maligned witch caught a break every now and again.

The idea that those who practiced witchcraft were minions employed to do the devil's bidding took hold during biblical times. Along with this belief came the assertion that each one of these agents of the netherworld boasted a mark that had been bestowed upon them by their diabolical leader.

The most prominent of these identifiers was a wart strategically placed on either the tip of their nose or on their chin. Any woman seen with a wart jutting from her face was given a wide berth, unless of course there happened to be a hair growing out of it since, as was previously mentioned, witches can't grow hair.

Along with the ever-popular wart, it was thought that witches were branded somewhere on their person with a mark that became known as the 'sign of the witch.' This skin discoloration was said to be oblivious to pain and completely devoid of blood.

During the Salem witch trials, if a birthmark or any other unusual blemish was visible on a suspected practitioner of the dark arts, a pin was used to prick the site. If it bled, this helped the beleaguered woman's case. If it didn't, this was regarded as irrefutable proof that the accused bore the mark of Satan and was, therefore, a true witch.

Witches have a reputation for surrounding themselves with a wide variety of non-human companions; their most favored of these being cats. Some believe that this is due to the feline's purported ability to easily navigate both the world of the living and that of the dead with ease. In times gone by, although innocent on the surface, this alliance was seen as having ominous undertones.

In the 17the century, a woman who kept company with a large assortment of cats was viewed with a mixture of fear and contempt. Many who saw evil where none existed assumed that a collector of felines was up to no good.

Rumor had it that cats who congregated around a witch were not cats at all, but rather the captured souls of those who had crossed her path and not lived to tell the tale. These victimized spirits, returned to earth in feline form, were fated to spend eternity at their tormentor's beck and call.

Today, a woman or man with an affinity for cats is not given a second thought. Centuries ago, in areas where overzealous imaginations ran rampant, a person's love of felines would have been enough to put them on the radar of those hell-bent on sending suspected witches to the gallows.

The saying "Money is the root of all evil" is one that witches of old apparently took to heart. So potent was its power that it was once believed that witches would cower in the presence of any form of currency.

This concept was so widespread that villagers in parts of Europe and the Thirteen Colonies would often scatter money around their beds at night in order to keep witches from preying on them as they slept. The theory behind this action was that a witch would be rendered powerless in the company of the ultimate symbol of evil.

This method of fighting fire with an even greater fire seemed to work. Spying the offensive items and finding herself unable to ply her trade, the dejected she-devil would beat a hasty retreat. Down, but not out, the night prowler would go in search of a home in which the occupants were lacking in funds, leaving their souls ripe for the taking.

While witches were thought to have strong bonds with cats, their relationship with dogs was another matter entirely. Back in the day, it was put forth that no practicing witch could be in the company of a canine for any length of time. Dogs, with their inborn ability to see past a person's exterior, could not only identify a witch on sight, but were also not shy about outing her to the world.

If was for this reason that people would turn a suspicious eye towards anyone for whom their dog had an aversion. Sensitive to the ways of evil, canines were said to be able to sense the essence of those they encountered. If an individual was pure of heart, the dog would accept them with nary a whimper. If, however, the animal smelled the stench of the devil on someone, they would react with apprehension, and on some occasions, unbridled aggression.

Since dogs, the most accepting of creatures, could supposedly detect malevolence in all its forms, their keen instincts were once used as tools to flush out witches masquerading as maidens. It was a time, to be sure, when falling out of grace with a dog could potentially land even the most pious of souls in hot water.

During the witch hunts that took place in various parts of Europe and the Americas in the 1600s, several methods were used to expose suspected practitioners. One of those was to take a woman who was accused of dabbling in witchcraft to a nearby lake or pond and submerge her in the water.

If the victim sank to the bottom, this was viewed as a favorable sign. If she rose to the top, her fate was sealed. Puritans believed that witches, owing to their roles as disciples of the devil, could not be baptized. Since their souls were not saved, the water would reject their physical forms, sending them to the surface. If a targeted woman had the misfortune of floating to the top of the water, this was viewed as confirmation that she was indeed a witch and thus unworthy of the life she had been given.

The following offering is shared fairly often among farmers who keep horses on their property. It plays into the fear that entities who dwell in the space between our world and the shadowlands are always closer than we think.

Supposedly, if a horse is found at sunrise with its mane a tangled mess, this means that a witch or other agent of darkness has ridden the animal during the night. Some believe that the dread experienced by the unwilling equine manifests in its tresses being left in a state of disarray. Others assert that the knotted condition of the mane is the result of the mysterious rider having used it in lieu of reins. Either way, it leaves a lasting impression on the horse who is never the same after spending the night in the company of witches.

My apologies in advance for this next entry which some might find a bit risqué. The image of a witch riding on a broomstick is the product of folklore at its finest. Although it's a pretty sure bet that witches throughout the ages utilized the same methods of transport as everyone else, somewhere along the line, they gained a reputation as broom riders.

Most people would agree that, realistically speaking, the only way to make a broom airborne is to throw it or drop it from a substantial height. The thought that someone, no matter their hidden talents, could take to the skies while sitting astride one of these cleaning implements is preposterous by anyone's standards. Even so, depictions of witches riding brooms have been around since the 1400s.

Although many theories have been batted around as to how this notion came about, one stands out from the rest. As strange as it sounds, it makes as much sense as anything else.

Since witches were viewed as independent entities who refused to take guff from anyone, their penchant for broom riding was said to be rooted in their need to establish dominance over a patriarchy that sought to rule, not only women, but anyone they viewed as inferior.

In an attempt to assert their power, it was believed that witches would straddle these long wooden sticks as a way of announcing, without ever uttering a word, that they were the ones in control. While this action had absolutely nothing to do with flying, it certainly explains the imagery behind it.

Chapter 12:

The Human Body

Some people claim that their bodies can predict the weather. When rain or a sudden cold snap is on the way, they say that their knees are aware of this long before the local meteorologist. If you happen to be one of those folks who believe the old wives' tale that a worsening of your aches and pains can be chalked up to changes in the atmosphere, science would have you know that the jury is still out on that one.

A controlled study of nearly twelve million Medicare patients found that complaints of excessive pain in the joints and bones of participants were actually greater in number when the weather was dry. Although the margin was negligible, it was enough to convince researchers that our bodies react pretty much the same regardless of weather conditions.

Now, people who suffer from arthritis and other ailments will be quick to tell you that the study is dead wrong. They will swear that their backs or necks become painful prior to and during a cloudburst. While some scientists proclaim that these symptoms would be present regardless of what is happening outside the window, those suffering from a touch of bursitis would beg to differ.

Conversely, in other studies, it has been proven that excessive temperatures and damp weather do indeed bring with them an increased level of discomfort; something that any old wife worth her salt already new.

As a child, you were probably cautioned on more than one occasion to bundle up before going outside so you wouldn't catch a cold. It stands to reason that venturing out into the frigid air would fill your lungs with an icy influx that would subsequently lead to sickness. As sound as that theory may be, much like the previous offering, a good bit of doubt has been cast on its validity.

Keeping your body temperature regulated boosts the immune system, of that there is no doubt. This is why we are advised to wear layers of clothing when the barometer drops. While this may make us more comfortable, it does nothing to prevent us from contracting the sniffles.

Since the common cold is a virus, it enters our systems through contact with the bacteria-laden droplets of those who carry the infection. Contrary to the teachings of many an old wife, the weather—hot, cold or otherwise—can't be blamed for your stuffy nose or racking cough. If this is indeed the case, the next time you're down with a cold, you can thank a walking germ machine instead of Mother Nature for your malady, or so they say.

We all know how painful it can be to stub one of our toes on a piece of furniture or other obstacle. What we don't realize as we nurse our aching appendage is that our clumsy action was actually some unseen force's way of telling us that we were headed someplace we were not meant to be. Rather than allowing us to continue on and face whatever catastrophe is lying in wait, fate throws something in our path, not to cause us harm, but to save us from the greater threat up ahead.

The belief that gazing at the Sun will make you sneeze is an old wives' tale that some people swear by. Unlike some far-fetched notions, this one is a real phenomenon that affects around a third of the Earth's population.

As it turns out, the sneezing fit that is sometimes brought on by the Sun is a reflex action that occurs when the bright light enters the eye, causing our pupils to constrict. When this happens, the trigeminal nerve is triggered which in turn irritates the sinus passages causing us to sneeze. These nerve endings, which don't normally interact, work in unison when confronted with the powerful rays of the bright star.

Tinnitus is a medical condition in which the sufferer's ears ring for a variety of reasons. In the land of superstitions, this nuisance has an explanation that some might view as bordering on paranoia.

Purportedly, if our ears start to buzz for no apparent reason it means that we are, at that very moment, the topic of someone's conversation. While this probably occurs more often than we would like to believe, if what's being said is positive, our ears can't detect it and stay quiet. If, however, the utterings are malicious in nature, our auditory senses perk up and take notice. Able to detect activity from afar, our ears sound an alarm, ringing loudly in an attempt to drown out the unkind words being spoken.

On a positive note, if our ears suddenly feel warm for no apparent reason, someone is speaking of us in glowing terms. Sensing this, they tingle as a way of letting us know that someone, somewhere, thinks that we are the bee's knees.

If your palm begins to itch for no apparent reason, get ready because your fortunes are about to change.

Whether this turns out to be good news or bad depends entirely upon where the irritation is located.

To develop a sudden itch on your right palm suggests that you can look forward to coming into a tidy sum of cash. The more intense the sensation, the larger the impending reward. Conversely, if your left hand is overcome by a persistent tickle, your bank account is about to take a hit. In this instance, rather than receiving money, you will be handing it over to someone else.

If both palms itch simultaneously, you will experience an unexpected gain that will soon be put to use out of necessity. While it may not be the outcome you were hoping for, there are worse things in life than breaking even.

Prickly palms are also believed to be an indicator that you are about to shake hands with someone who will become a meaningful influence in your life. Just be careful not to scratch that itch, to do so will negate the good fortune that fate had in store.

Even those who don't normally entertain superstitions are sometimes guilty of crossing their fingers to help ensure that something they long for comes to pass. For reasons that aren't entirely clear, it is believed that crossing your fingers while uttering a wish out loud prevents mischievous sprites that may be lurking nearby from hearing your desires and squelching them before they become reality.

It has been speculated that the action of crossing one finger over another is done in an attempt to approximate a crucifix. By making this gesture, a person is calling upon divine forces to combat opportunistic entities whose intentions are anything but pure.

It is also thought that white lies will be forgiven if the teller crosses their fingers as the half-truths are being spoken. This too is believed to harken back to the power of the True Cross. By crossing their fingers, those with a tendency to fib are secretly asking a higher power to overlook their transgression.

At the end of the day, whether a person is wishing for something that lies just beyond their reach or signaling to be let off the hook for spinning a yarn they know to be false, crossing their fingers should do the trick. It would seem that some superstitions, such as this one, are more versatile than others.

SUPERSTITIONS, OLD WIVES' TALES, & FOLKLORE

Truth be told, when we are worn out from the drudgery of daily life or because we are sleep deprived, our bodies help us out by causing us to yawn which introduces an influx of oxygen into our blood streams, allowing us to feel momentarily rejuvenated.

For those who believe that even the most mundane action should be approached with caution, yawning is more than just an attempt to clear a foggy mind. These broad-thinkers will tell you that the act of opening your mouth involuntarily is brought about by the knowledge that, somewhere buried in your sixth sense, you are aware that someone has just spoken your name. Even though you neither heard nor saw this take place, you attempt to reply, but find yourself struck silent. The only thing you can manage in the moment is a deep inhalation of air followed by a slow exhalation.

These same people will also advise you to cover your mouth when you yawn, just as you do when you sneeze. If you don't, you set yourself up as a sitting duck for a roving demon that might see the opening and decide to dive right in. Once this nasty specimen has entered your body, a world of turmoil lay ahead. From then on, you will spend your days aware that you are no longer yourself, but powerless to do anything about it. According to lore, the portal that was created by the yawn would have been inaccessible had you only made an effort to suppress your yawn.

Clipping our nails is not an enjoyable task, but a necessary one nonetheless. For those who believe in serendipity, the time of day in which we choose to undertake this chore can make the difference between a life on easy street and a flood of bad luck that leaves us gasping for air.

If you trim your nails in the daylight, you have nothing to worry about. For those who prefer to tackle this tedious task after the sun goes down, a world of hurt is said to lie ahead. The act of removing these overgrown bits of keratin at a time when the ghastly things that prowl the night are out in force is akin to inviting them to destroy all that you have amassed. Attracted by the shedding of this once-living protein, they will surround you from that point on, allowing in only darkness as they keep all that is good at bay.

It is also believed that these same sinister entities will use the cut that is left behind in what remains of the nail as an access point into the body of the unsuspecting host. Once inside, they have the power to control the spirit of the luckless person whose only crime was choosing the wrong hour in which to groom their fingernails.

To cut your fingernails and toenails on the same day is an ill-advised endeavor. If you focus on only one or the other, providing that it is daytime, you will see an upturn in your fortunes. If you choose to get the job done all at once, the positive luck you invited is cancelled out by the negative energy produced when all of your nails were trimmed in one sitting. While not the worst possible outcome, it does mean that any windfall or joyous news that was coming your way will now be tempered with a bout of misfortune.

If you find yourself being overcome by a sudden sneezing fit, and are not suffering from a cold or other respiratory ailment, you just might be preying on someone's mind. This could be taken as an insult, a boon to your ego, or a gift from your immortal soul, depending on the circumstances.

To sneeze one time and be done with it suggests that someone is talking about you in less-than-glowing terms. So palpable is their vitriol that it builds up in your body and must then be expelled.

If you sneeze twice, a person you haven't seen in a while misses you with all their being. These feelings of longing are so intense that they are magically parlayed to you in the form of a sneeze.

Three sneezes in a row indicate that you have a secret admirer. Even though you may be completely unaware of their existence, they pine for you from afar.

Multiple sneezes mean that you have been thinking impure thoughts that border on evil. In an attempt to cleanse your physical form, your soul induces a barrage of sneezing, forcing you to expel the wicked notions that have polluted your mind and body.

When babies and small children get the hiccups, parents often joke that their little ones are growing. When adults are overcome with these sometimes uncomfortable muscle spasms, it's not nearly as cute or funny.

Hiccups can occur for a variety of reasons, none of which are a precursor to a growth spurt. Wolfing down food or indulging in a bubbly beverage can introduce air and gas into our systems that agitate our diaphragms, resulting in a bout of hiccups.

In some cultures, hiccups are thought to mean that the sufferer is monopolizing the thoughts of another. Normally, this is taken as a sign that a person in whom you have a romantic interest feels the same way and can't stop thinking about you.

For those who see everything as a negative, a sudden bout of hiccups indicates that someone known to the afflicted party is thinking of them with contempt. So palpable is their spite that it manifests in the form of hiccups.

Chapter 13:

Love, Sweet Love

Some people prefer to sit in the aisle seat in a movie theater or on an airplane. While this might be a practical choice for those who enjoy easy access of movement, unless they wish to spend their lives alone, they may want to rethink their position.

To sit in solitude sends the message to the powers-that-be that you prefer your own company to that of others. While this may be well and good in the interim, it doesn't bode well for those who desire to someday find a mate.

Likewise, if a person reserves a table for one in a restaurant, they have announced to the universe that they are happy being alone. Since the eyes and ears of fate are always upon us, our wish is their command. If we are constantly making it clear that we want to be left on our own, they will make it happen—with a vengeance.

For those who are unattached at the moment, but hope to find everlasting love at some point in the future, they would do well to mingle rather than set themselves apart. Not only are they more apt to meet a kindred spirit, but their actions also help to inform any unseen busybodies who might be watching that they are not solitary beings. Once their position is made clear, the love they seek will find them.

There are several superstitions revolving around pearls, one of the sea's most coveted treasures. What these beliefs mean for those hoping to find love is almost entirely dependent upon the gem's color and whether it was purchased or given as a gift.

White pearls, according to Greek mythology, represent the tears shed by Aphrodite, the goddess of love, after her heart was broken by an unfaithful paramour. From that point on, if a woman was gifted white pearls, any romantic relationships she pursued were doomed to end badly.

There was, however, a way around this unpleasant outcome. If the recipient of the pearls offered the giver a few coins in exchange, her love life would take a turn for the better. Having purchased the pearls outright, she had avoided offending the gods and therefore would find happiness in the arms of the next person who caught her fancy.

If a single female is given black pearls on a special occasion, she will soon find herself being showered with attention from a number of eligible suitors. These heavily pigmented gems are symbols of love and devotion and can be gifted without worry. To receive black pearls is to know that your soulmate is nearby and will find you when the time is right.

Rabbits are soft, fluffy, timid, and all around adorable. They are also, as most of us know, somewhat randy and exceedingly fertile. Their reputations as rapid reproducers make them perfect fodder for superstitions that promote love in all its forms.

It is believed that if a couple who are courting happen to encounter a wild rabbit that shows no fear of humans, this suggests that they are destined to spend the rest of their lives together. Not only will they marry and live happily ever after, but they can also expect to fill their home with children.

If a lone individual comes across a rabbit that seems to be studying them intensely, that person has recently met their soulmate, or soon will. As a result of the encounter, the union foreseen by the prolific animal will be fruitful, producing a large number of offspring.

So, if you ever find yourself being judged by an oddly curious rabbit at a time when your love life is struggling, take it as a sign that you are about to be struck by Cupid's arrow. If, however, you cross paths with such a creature, but are not yet ready to settle down and start a family, you might want to make a quick detour. To tarry just might put you on the client list of nature's most notorious matchmaker.

Most of us have broken a cup or other household item at one time or another. When these mishaps occur, rather than throwing the fragments away, it is tempting to reach for the glue and attempt to repair the damage. As superstition has it, this often futile effort can lead to the fracturing of the relationships of those living in the home.

Objects that are broken into numerous pieces, no matter how sentimental they may be to the owner, should be thrown out immediately. Not only are they considered to be bad luck in general, but the cracks and shattered bits are said to mimic the lives of the people around them.

Once something is broken beyond repair, it can never be made whole again. Even though it may come close, the cracks will remain visible. In lore, these fissures are thought to represent the hearts of those who share space with the imperfect item.

If a couple resides in the home, as the seams deepen, so too will the space between them. As time passes, the patchwork will crumble, destroying both the knick-knack and the relationship it has come to symbolize.

If the broken item is a picture frame that holds the image of the main pairing in the residence, their union is destined to fail if the frame is not replaced with a new one post haste. Any attempt to make the splintered piece whole again will end badly for all those involved.

Having scissors slip from your grasp can be dangerous for reasons other than the obvious. Lore dictates that if a woman drops a pair of scissors, this indicates that her significant other is seeing someone else behind her back. The secret the lothario carries, coupled with the fear of what might happen if the truth comes to light prompts his subconscious to do everything in its power to keep sharp objects out of the hands of the one he is betraying.

In order to put an end to his two-timing without causing a scene, the put upon partner can sew the feather of a monogamous bird, such as a mourning dove, owl or swan inside the pillow on which her lover sleeps. From then on, as he slumbers, he will be reminded that faithfulness is a virtue not to be taken lightly.

After several nights spent with his head resting upon the feather, the cheater will reach an epiphany. Upon recognizing the error of his ways, he will vow from that moment on to remain true to the person with whom he shares the bed.

Just as a broken furnishing is believed by some to foretell the future state of a relationship, so too does the fraying of clothing worn by the parties involved. This is why pulling on a string that has begun to unravel from a garment is considered tantamount to ringing the death knell for a romantic pairing.

Apparently, nearly everything around us has at least some influence on the status of our love lives, including the clothes on our backs. If these articles begin to unravel, this is believed to be providence's way of telling us that the hold we once had on the one we adore is waning. As the garment falls apart, bit by bit, the feelings we once shared follow suit. If the loose strings are cut away, this only serves to prolong the inevitable. It would seem that, once the process has begun, there is no way to turn things around. Thankfully, however, all hope is not lost.

It is held that if the garment is destroyed in its entirety before the flaw is allowed to gain momentum, the events that would have taken place are halted in their infancy. Rather than ending the relationship, the action signals a time of rebirth from which the union emerges stronger than ever.

Chapter 14:

Vampire Lore

Although it may not be apparent to those who live in noisy cities, country dwellers know well when night is about to fall. It is not only the vision of the Sun setting on the horizon that gives them a heads-up, but also the cries of the nocturnal creatures that have awoken to greet the darkness. These worshippers of the Moon take great pleasure in announcing that, for the time being, they are the eyes of the world.

If you've ever wondered how vampires know when it's time to rise and shine, here's one possible answer. Awakened by the music of the crickets, owls and frogs that inhabit the twilight, vampires emerge from their dens, or coffins, and venture into the shadows to feed. While Mother Nature is known to provide wake-up calls for those who walk during the day, it would seem that she does the same for the nefarious ilk that stalk the hours from dusk till dawn.

The mystery of how a person becomes a vampire in the first place has lingered in the minds of believers for centuries. While it is widely presumed that this transformation occurs when someone who is afflicted feeds on a mortal victim, but spares their life, there are other ways that are fabled to lead to this nearly inescapable state of non-being.

One suspected means of being ushered into the world of the undead is to have a cat jump onto a casket that is destined for the graveyard. When this happens, the corpse being housed inside will rise shortly thereafter in the form of a vampire. Along those same lines, a cat crossing the path of a funeral procession will have similar results.

Those who choose to end their lives prematurely are said to be punished for their action by being returned to the world they attempted to escape, this time in the guise of a vampire. Rather than finding the peace they were hoping for, these lost souls are forced to walk the earth for eternity. The misery they experienced in life will remain with them as they journey through the millenniums in a state of perpetual sadness.

It is common knowledge that silver can kill a werewolf, but what effect does it have on vampires? While not lethal, it is believed that silver bullets have the power to inflict serious injuries, including paralysis, upon these normally impervious entities.

Apparently, the natural elements found in pure silver do not sit well in a vampire's system. When introduced in any form, the metal causes a burning sensation that can last for several hours, or days, depending on the level of exposure.

Another explanation is that vampires loathe the purity that silver represents. When in its presence, they are so repulsed by the unsullied nature of the substance that they must flee or risk exposing their true face.

In Greek mythology, Artemis, the goddess of the hunt and overseer of wildlife, was said to have happened upon a vampire as he was attempting to pilfer her collection of silver. Furious, she laid a curse on the interloper and all his kind. From that day forward, any vampire who came in contact with silver would suffer burns as retribution for the actions of the would-be thief.

The most effective tool that can be used to ward off a suspected vampire is a silver crucifix. Its representation of the holiest of figures, combined with its elemental composition, makes the object unbearable to vampires. When placed upon the skin of a creature of the night, the burn that is left behind will remain forever, thus branding the subject as one who feasts upon the blood of the living.

Garlic is thought to be as much of a nuisance to vampires as the aforementioned silver. Although not nearly as potent, the smell and taste of the savory cloves are enough to keep even the most determined fiend at a distance.

In the early 1800s, garlic was heavily consumed by people who made their livings working the fields. Through trial and error, they discovered that, as pleasant as the taste was to most humans, creatures hungering for a blood meal avoided it like the plague. It soon became evident that pesky mosquitos and biting flies would rather starve than feed off of anyone whose insides were polluted with garlic.

Vampires were counted among those who would steer clear of garlic at all cost. Since they were bloodsuckers as well, to smell garlic on a potential victim was an unmistakable warning to keep away. To take one bite was to risk introducing the pungent vegetable into their system, something no vampire would ever do willingly.

Vampires subsist on blood, that much is a given. As it happens, the source of this precious commodity is as important to their longevity as sleeping during the day and avoiding the objects meant to do them harm.

One hard and fast rule is that vampires cannot survive by feeding from others of their kind. Contrary to some Hollywood depictions, the undead require certain elements that can only be found in the blood of humans. While they can theoretically drink from another vampire, the action is likened to sipping from an empty glass; they get nothing out of it.

Likewise, although they can purportedly get by on the blood of non-human animals, the experience is less than satisfying. The substituted cells will sustain their existence, but leave them constantly lacking.

Even though humans are their ideal prey, vampires must be choosy when it comes to procuring a meal. For example, someone who is ailing is not a good candidate for obvious reasons. While the malady from which they suffer cannot be passed directly to the feeder, the offering is often distasteful and lacking in the nutrients they crave.

In the end, vampires, like most other species, will consume whatever is available in order to survive. With that said, they tend to be a tad more finicky than other creatures of lore.

It is a well-known assertion that vampires do not cast reflections in glass or mirrors. This is not surprising since they lack a core of humanity. It has been speculated that mirrors cannot display images of non-living entities that have shunned the light for the darkness.

Another theory as to why vampires fail to appear in reflective surfaces is rooted in times gone by. In the old days, looking glasses were often backed with unadulterated silver, an element that was previously mentioned as being abhorred by the undead.

Silver, particularly when used in the construction of anything that reflects light, was believed to have the power to absorb evil. This knowledge resulted in vampires avoiding mirrors whenever possible, lest their essence be pulled inside and held in limbo for eternity.

Anyone who has watched horror movies with vampires at their center, knows that exposure to sunlight will result in a fiery death for these night stalkers. While this means of eliminating blood feeders is almost universally accepted as foolproof, there are loopholes to consider.

When they are in human form, vampires are vulnerable to ultraviolet rays, especially those which emanate directly from the Sun. There is, however, a way around this for those who wish to inhabit the world of the living anytime they please without forfeiting their immortality in the process.

Utilizing their talent for shapeshifting, vampires can transform themselves into beings that are impervious to daylight. While they have the ability to assume any identity of their choosing, their preferred personas are thought to be those of bats and wolves. While in these guises, vampires can scout prey without raising the suspicions of those around them.

In bygone eras, when a nocturnal animal was found roaming the countryside in the light of day, residents would scramble for ways to explain the creature's uncharacteristic behavior. Although their presence raised some eyebrows, only those whose lives were steeped in folklore viewed it as a sign that a vampire had found its way into their midst.

One of the most universally accepted ways to destroy a vampire is to drive a stake through its heart while it is indisposed. In this case, it is not the implement that is important, but the material from which it is fashioned.

Vampires are said to possess a natural fear of wood. This notion, if accurate, can be traced back to biblical times. Since the undead detest any tools of Christianity, it is believed that they recoil at the sight of wood, the God-given material used to construct the cross on which Christ was crucified.

To have a stake carved from wood, particularly that of a dogwood tree, plunged into their heart will end a vampire's reign of terror in short order. The trauma, coupled with the representation of the messiah, is something no blood feeder can withstand. It is also for this reason that wooden crosses often grace churches and homes. Not only are they lethal to vampires, but they also have the power to ward off evil in all its forms.

It has been established that vampires recoil at the sight of a crucifix, cannot be seen in mirrors, abhor sunlight, and detest garlic. To add to this list, it is also alleged that these clever beings are equipped with the ability to suppress their urge to sprout fangs and feed on everything that moves the moment that night falls. It is thought that, out of necessity, they have become masters at keeping their condition under wraps, thus ensuring their survival as a species.

If someone has a feeling that a vampire has somehow infiltrated their life, not that this is a common occurrence in most circles, there is a non-confrontational way of outing the suspect. In order to force a vampire to give up the ghost, so to speak, one need only tie a string, rope, scarf, or any other item of substantial length in a series of knots and leave it out in the open for all to see.

Vampires have a reputation for being unable to resist the urge to untie knots and will immediately set about untangling the mess that has been left out as bait. Since most people take little pleasure in such a bothersome task, if a guest to your home spies a knotted object and cannot be persuaded to leave it be, you would do well to show them the door before they turn their attention to more delectable game.

Ever since the days of Bela Lugosi, vampires have been depicted as sensual beings whose prowess does not end with the hunt. The reality, if we're being honest, is probably nowhere near as titillating as we have been led to believe.

Vampires, being dead and all, are unlikely to be in the market for romantic entanglements. With their existence ruled by an insatiable desire to feed, they hardly have time for liaisons with the living. Although the idea plays well in books and on the big screen, it's doubtful that, if vampires do roam among us, they are looking for brief encounters.

Putting all that aside, the practicality of such endeavors comes into question. Since vampires no longer have need of normal human functions, this makes it unlikely that they bow to the whims of their non-existent hormones. Assuming that they were born human, the qualities they once boasted are long gone, including the ability to consume any form of nourishment other than blood products. Why then would they harbor romantic feelings or the ability to act upon those emotions should the need arise?

This is, of course, merely conjecture born of equal parts curiosity and physiology. Perhaps these bloodthirsty entities are indeed the peerless lovers they are reputed to be in literature and on celluloid. When all is said and done, their libidos, or lack thereof, only add to the allure of the enigmatic vampire.

Chapter 15:

Old Wives' Tales Involving Food

Freshly baked bread is a temptation few can resist. Every now and again, however, when slicing into the luscious loaf, a sizable hole can be found running through the middle. For most of us, this simply means that the dough wasn't prepped properly, allowing gas to become trapped in the center. Those who believe wholeheartedly in their old auntie's somewhat skewed take on everyday events know better. To them, this empty space is a cryptic message from beyond.

According to this foreboding little anecdote, a tunnel inside a loaf of bread represents the hole in the ground that will someday hold the remains of the one whose hands formed the dough. To make matters worse for the ill-fated confectioner, the larger the space, the closer they are to the grave.

Using apples to determine the identity of a future mate is a bit of folklore that is somewhat sweet, much like the fruit itself. It involves, not the juicy flesh, but its insightful outer covering.

As the story goes, if a maiden (sorry guys, for whatever reason this works only for those of the female persuasion) is able to pare an apple in one continuous strip, she will be given a clue to the name of the person she will someday marry.

Anyone who has ever peeled an apple, or any fruit for that matter, knows how difficult it is to do so without hacking it to pieces. While that's as may be, if a woman possesses the dexterity needed to accomplish this feat, she will be rewarded handsomely for her efforts.

Once the deed is done, the skilled damsel must then turn around three times and toss the peeling onto a flat surface. The cursive letter that it most resembles will be the first initial of her future beau's forename. If no letter can be deciphered, the hopeful lover will remain forever single. While they may be succulent, apples, as history has proven time and again, can be merciless when it comes to matters of the heart.

Few people deliberately swallow the seeds of fruits such as watermelons and pumpkins. That being said, occasionally one slips down your gullet before you know it. When this happens, since what has occurred cannot be undone, we continue enjoying our snack without a care in the world. That is, unless we're familiar with a cautionary bit of old wives' wisdom that warns of the dangers these innocuous-looking seeds pose to the human body if consumed whole.

To swallow a seed, on purpose or by accident, is to set off a chain of events that never end well for the person who set the scenario in motion. They will know something is wrong a few hours after the incident when their tummy begins to rumble and ache. Acting under the assumption that something they consumed didn't agree with them, they take a tablet of some sort to ease their discomfort, usually washing it down with a glass of water. This, as it happens, is their second mistake.

Unbeknownst to the sufferer, the seed they swallowed has begun to sprout inside their belly. Having given it the water it needed in order to grow, the resulting vines fill the gut before branching out into other areas of their abdomen. Within hours, the subject is rolling on the floor in agony as their body is consumed from the inside by the insidious plant.

This is nonsense, of course, given the highly acidic environment that exists in the human stomach. That being said, there was a well-documented case that took place in Massachusetts that closely mirrored this outlandish belief. It all began when an elderly man was enjoying some peas with his dinner. During the course of the meal, a pea went down the wrong pipe. After a brief coughing fit, he regained his composure and all seemed well.

A few weeks later, the man started having trouble breathing. Already suffering from several respiratory ailments, he made an appointment with his doctor just to be on the safe side. Upon examining the fellow, it was discovered that a pea plant had taken root in his lung. Fortunately, the sprout was removed and the patient walked away unscathed. It can be presumed that in the aftermath of his ordeal, he probably learned to chew his food carefully before swallowing.

Having food leftover at the end of a meal is not a crime. However, neglecting to place these leavings in the refrigerator or bin is on par with one if you believe in certain antiquated customs. In lore, leaving a plate of food out in the open overnight is an invitation for the devil to make himself at home. Called forth by the aroma of spoiling fare, the lord of the underworld will dine at your expense, in more ways than one.

Cheese, whether hard and sharp or creamy and gooey, is a food lover's dream come true. Yes, it is also high in cholesterol and a clogged artery waiting to happen, but most of us are willing to take that risk if it means indulging in its rich goodness.

Health hazards aside, it is fabled that if you consume cheese before retiring for the night, you will be plagued by horrifying nightmares until sunrise. While this may seem a bit extreme, the belief does have some medical merit. It seems that the chemical makeup of cheese can wreak havoc with our serotonin levels, resulting in insomnia and restless sleep.

On a more positive note, there are those who believe that the rich fat content in cheese, specifically the softer varieties—ironically—increase a man's virility. A fellow wishing to sow his wild oats need only fill up on his favorite cheese in preparation for the big event. Infused with vigor courtesy of the milk curds, his talents will be unmatched.

Whether you are suffering from the common cold, the flu or just about any other malady known to man, chicken soup has a reputation as the one food with the power to get you back on your feet in no time. Surprisingly, this isn't far from the truth.

Broth and chicken alone are thought to be helpful in relieving sinus congestion, mainly due to the steam that rises from the concoction which helps to clear your airways. If carrots, onions, garlic, celery and potatoes are added to the mix, the cure factor rises considerably. Loaded with vitamins and minerals, these healthy ingredients boost the immune system, paving the way for wellness.

Chapter 16:

The Mythology of Wolves

Wolves, the shadows of the forest, hold a special place in folklore. These intelligent, enigmatic creatures inspire both awe and fear in all they behold.

Wolves are judged for a variety of reasons, one of those being the color of their fur. A white wolf is considered an agent of light that has been sent from the heavens to tend the sheep which, metaphorically speaking, are us.

Black wolves are the antithesis of their pale brethren. These purveyors of darkness are the devil's eyes on earth. As they observe us from afar, so too does the atrocity that orchestrates their every move.

To see black and white wolves congregating together means that both sides have their sights set on you. This is thought to be an indication that whatever path you are currently on will ultimately lead to your downfall. The presence of these opposing symbols is intended to put you on the straight and narrow before it's too late. If you choose to turn your life around for the better, the white wolf has won. If you go the other way, its formidable counterpart will return for you at a later date. You will then be escorted to the netherworld where an eternity of torment awaits.

Humans are a wolf's natural enemy. If one of these shy creatures shows no fear in the presence of this obvious threat, it is taken as a sign that the animal is actually a spirit in disguise. Neither good nor evil, these grey ghosts are merely lost souls returned to earth to spend time among the living while keeping their true identity hidden.

If you are ever lucky enough to see three wolves together, don't get too excited. This encounter, while memorable, suggests that you will never marry or find love. You will instead be relegated to a life of solitude and loneliness, much like the tagalong third wolf.

Wolves are apex predators that instill dread in their prospective prey. The stink of fear on livestock that have survived a wolf attack is said to be so strong that they are summarily ostracized by others of their kind. The scent of the wolf that remains never dissipates, causing other animals to avoid the creature that managed to get away. Even though it may have temporarily outsmarted death, the ill-fated survivor is reminded with every minute that passes that something sinister is nearby and will come back for it someday.

While wolves will normally go out of their way to avoid humans, they still hold power over us, whether we know it or not. If you hear one of these magnificent creatures howling on your birthday, for instance, they're letting you know that you should make the most of the day. Unfortunately, this gesture is done, not out of respect, but out of pity. Privy to that which occurs in the world that lies just beyond our own, they know something you don't know, namely that this birthday will be your last.

It is well-known that wolves are loners that stay out of sight as much as possible, especially when humans are around. So obsessive is their need to fly under the radar that they supposedly have the power to erase the memory of anyone who comes upon them by accident.

In extreme cases, it is believed that wolves will drive the observer mad to ensure that their whereabouts remain hidden. In the 18th and 19th centuries, men would occasionally go missing during hunting expeditions, only to turn up days, or even weeks later claiming that they had no recollection of the events leading up to their return to society. With no explanations at hand, it was speculated that they had encountered wolves that had stripped them of their memories in order to protect the pack.

In parts of Asia, wolves are viewed as protectors of both man and beast. Considered good luck charms, they are a welcome presence on farms dependent on the land to survive. Although predators themselves, wolves that take up residence near a farm are thought to keep nuisance animals away from crops and livestock.

Besides their usefulness at keeping the deer and hare populations down, wolves are also thought to ward off evil spirits who attempt to enter through portals undetectable to humans, but obvious to wildlife. Rumored to be masters in the art of shapeshifting, wolves are adept at playing both sides of the eternal fence.

On top of keeping evil entities at arm's length, wolves are also a known enemy of witches. In Serbian mythology, overprotective parents would often name their children Vuk, or wolf, in order to fool witches who supposedly preyed upon the innocent. Even the most determined practitioner of the dark arts would put space between themselves and any home they believed to be inhabited by a Vuk.

Chapter 17:

Strange Beliefs about Animals

In the realm of superstitions, encountering a white animal that is normally pigmented can be either a lucky fluke or a recipe for disaster, depending on the situation.

To stumble upon a white snake in the wild suggests that you are a pure soul who is destined to lead a blessed life. If the snake remains still, your future is on the right track. If it quickly moves to another location, this is a sign that you need to make some changes if you want your dreams to come true.

Since we're on the subject, given that it was a snake that supposedly tricked Eve into taking a bite of the forbidden apple, it has long-been assumed that these reptiles are on the devil's payroll. The fact that they tend to live underground only adds to their less than admirable reputation.

In folklore, snakes travel back and forth between earth and Hades at will. As favored children of the underworld, they have been given the ability to cause decomposition in the living. This is evident in the necrosis that often occurs in the aftermath of a bite from a venomous snake. The rotting tissue at the site of the wound is said to simulate the breakdown of flesh that takes place after death.

While most of us have heard that it is bad luck to have a black cat cross our path, to have a white one step in front of us signals that good fortune lay ahead. If a snowy feline is overly affectionate towards a total stranger, the charmed recipient can expect a windfall within days of the interaction.

To see a white owl perched near your home in the light of day is to court misfortune. If it, or any other bird, makes its way into a residence and lands on a bed, death waits around the corner for the person who last slept on the ill-fated piece of furniture.

If a white animal shows up at a graveside funeral, this indicates that either the decedent or someone interred nearby has joined the proceedings. If the unexpected guest departs before the ceremony is complete, so too has the soul it personified.

To do harm to a white animal is considered by some to be a mortal sin. In 1913, Austria's Archduke Franz Ferdinand, an avid hunter, happened upon a rare white deer while on a routine hunt. Seizing this once-in-a-lifetime opportunity, he took its life without a moment's hesitation.

Those closest to him later claimed that he was stricken with regret almost instantly. Knowing full-well that there was a curse associated with killing a white animal, he became obsessed with the notion that his impulsive action would hasten his demise.

Less than a year later, Ferdinand and his wife Sophie were felled by an assassin's bullets while riding in a motorcade through the streets of Sarajevo. This tragedy would prove to be the spark that helped ignite the First World War, leading many to wonder if the monumental events that followed were set in motion, not on the battlefield, but on a hunting trip. Anything is possible given the belief that within every superstition lay a modicum of truth.

Goats have the unfortunate distinction of being considered representatives of the devil, due mostly to their depictions in literature and on film. These strong-willed creatures are thought to not only attract evil, but to feed off of it.

In contrast, these same animals are believed by some to act as buffers against the very thing they reputedly thrive on. It is said that if a goat walks ahead of you, they will swallow any malevolent energies that might be present. Since they have no fear of such things and consume them at every opportunity, with a goat leading the way, the human soul remains untouched by the hand of evil.

A rabbit that appears on a forest path with an apparent injury is not always what it seems. As the story goes, these timid, non-threatening creatures may actually be witches in disguise. It is believed that this pathetic ruse is used to lure travelers off the road and deep into the woods. Once they reach the witch's lair, her secret is revealed. Finding themselves at her mercy, the victims of the trickery are never seen or heard from again.

By the same token, unclean spirits are said to sometimes take a page from the book of witches by assuming the outer form of a rabbit in an attempt to infiltrate homes. Soon after adopting the role of family pet, these fiendish entities begin manipulating those around them. When the world they once knew crumbles, the hapless victims never suspect that their downfall was orchestrated by their floppy-eared companion.

On a lighter note, animal lore isn't always foreboding. To see a plump rabbit, for example, simply means that you would do well to stockpile firewood in preparation for an exceedingly cold winter.

If birds are seen flying low to the ground, this suggests that a storm is coming.

If you ever find yourself lost in an area where horses roam free, observe them closely if you wish to survive. Horses, in their wisdom, will not consume tainted water. Therefore, if you need to quench your thirst, drink from the same source as a horse; they will never steer you wrong.

Every now and then, news outlets will feature stories detailing sightings of pink dolphins in the world's oceans. These marine mammals, while magnificent to be sure, have a special place in animal lore, not only for their unusual appearance, but also for their similarities to mermaids.

Pink dolphins are believed to have been human at one time. Banished to the sea for reasons only they would know, they swim the oceans during the day. At nightfall, they emerge from the water in human form. While on land, they are said to roam local villages until sunrise in search of children to take with them when they return to the ocean. What they do with those they abduct is a mystery. Perhaps they too transition into lifeforms that dwell in the water by day and on land when the Moon lights the sky.

If you like to fish and want to take home a sizable bounty, be sure to throw back the first catch of the day. This act of respect is smiled upon by the keepers of the water who will then reward you with a plentiful supply of fish. It is believed that once you've gained their trust, the water lords will generously provide for you in return.

Let's face it—rats have a bad reputation that they don't really deserve. Yes, they can spread disease and certainly aren't the cutest creatures ever created, but they have their good points. Intelligent beyond their station, rats are believed to have a sixth sense that allows them to see impending doom long before humans, and several other species that are held in high regard.

Witnessing a colony of rats running away in unison signals that they are fleeing from a threat that will bring devastation to all living things in its path. If you ever find yourself in this situation, you'd be wise to follow close behind since it is assumed that, more often than not, the lowly rats are leading the way to safety.

Chapter 18:

Oldies, But Goodies

Bread and butter is a cautionary notion that my mother still references anytime we are out together. The gist of this belief is that two people walking side-by-side should not be separated by anything in their path. To allow such a thing to occur will inevitably lead to their being parted on a more permanent basis.

For example, if a couple is walking hand-in-hand on the street and a lamppost or sign is up ahead, one of them has to blurt out "bread and butter" before they unlock hands to make way for the obstacle. This simple utterance ensures that the pair, although briefly parted, will remain bound together in spirit.

It isn't difficult to understand the logic behind this concept. Bread and butter are two things that are considered by most to be a natural pairing. By saying "bread and butter," two people who belong together are letting any negative presence that might be hovering nearby know that their parting is only temporary.

The lighting of candles is a common practice that is utilized during times of mourning, prayer, meditation, and relaxation. On the opposite end of the spectrum, candles also play a role in many rituals of a far darker nature.

There are several superstitions related to candles and, more specifically, their flames. It is believed that if a candle's flame suddenly changes from its normal hue to a deep blue, an uninvited guest has entered the room. Usually, this signifies the presence of something from the spirit world.

A flame that suddenly appears to reach for the ceiling is also a sign that an otherworldly being is present. If attempts to blow out the

SUPERSTITIONS, OLD WIVES' TALES, & FOLKLORE 101

candle fail repeatedly, this could mean that something from the other side is trying to make contact. In this instance, the spirit will attempt to thwart any efforts to extinguish the flame since doing so would sever their only line of communication.

A candle that continues to smoke long after the flame has been smothered is also representative of a lingering manifestation. It seems that, just as candles bring solace to the living, they do the same for those who reside in the land of shadows.

Another superstition that I have heard my whole life is that it is bad luck to watch someone leave until they disappear from sight. To do so signifies that they are walking out of your life for good, never to return.

My mother, to this day, will go to the window and wave to us as we are leaving, but will then retreat to her chair before we drive away. Since this acorn didn't fall far from the tree, I find myself turning my back before anyone I care about vanishes from my line of vision. After all, we can never be too careful when it comes to the safety of the ones we love.

One of the most lasting fears to be instilled in us as children was that of mysterious noises. A loud bang that seemed to emanate from everywhere and nowhere at once was the one that we came to dread more than any other.

I don't know if this is typical in all households, but every once in a while we would hear something that sounded like an extremely heavy object hitting the side of our house. Upon inspection, there would be no damage to be seen nor would we find anything lying around that didn't belong there. Although the sound had been deafening, the origins remained elusive.

As was to be expected, my mother took this as an omen of doom. Fearing the worst, she would be on pins and needles for days afterwards. In her experience, something terrible could be expected to happen within three days of the incident. This idea was one that had been passed down in her family for generations.

It was never fully explained, but I gathered that the loud whack was presumed to be the result of something trying to break through from the other side with a warning to tread lightly or face the consequences.

These disturbances were rare, but when they did occur, they brought our household to a standstill. Normally, three days would pass without incident and the whole thing would soon be forgotten. Still, every now and then, there would be an unpleasant episode that would bring the matter to a close.

In one instance, it was our cat being struck and killed by a car the day after we heard the bang that fulfilled the warning. As callous as it may sound, my mother commented that she hated what happened to our pet, but was glad that the ordeal was over so she could stop worrying.

I haven't heard the sound that used to rock our family home to its foundation since moving out on my own decades ago. Perhaps my mother was the catalyst since she had experienced the bizarre phenomena, in various places throughout her life.

Whether an unexpected sound that seems to come out of nowhere is indeed a heads-up from another realm or a completely benign natural occurrence is debatable. All I know is that, where I grew up, it was the former, without a shadow of doubt.

Walking under a ladder is considered bad luck for more reasons than one. For example, there is always the possibility that it could collapse, or that something being held by the person utilizing it at the time could fall, potentially injuring anyone standing below.

Besides these real-life dangers, ladders are also thought to represent something far more spiritual in nature. Some believe that the triangle formed by the ladder as it leans against a structure harkens back to the

Holy Trinity. To mindlessly infiltrate this space dedicated to the Father, Son, and Holy Ghost is seen as an act of disrespect that is punishable by a flood of misfortune that can last for several years.

To have a framed photo of a loved one fall off the wall is considered to be a sign that misfortune will settle upon at least one of the parties whose image appears behind the glass.

Likewise, to have a frame that is sitting on a flat surface suddenly topple forward is an ominous warning to whoever is depicted in the photo. If the glass portion of the frame cracks, this indicates that an ending of some sort is on the horizon.

If a couple appears in the photo, this signifies that an uncoupling is imminent. If a lone individual is in the picture, their days could be numbered. A group photo is a wild card. It is possible that bad luck will befall only one of those present when the image was captured. When this occurs, believers in such things are forced to wait with bated breath to find out who among them will be touched by the fickle hand of fate.

To mindlessly rock a vacant chair is believed by some to bring devastating consequences to the person who normally occupies the space. The practice is akin to proclaiming that they are no longer present in body, but now exist only in spirit. If the chair is not usually assigned to anyone in particular, then the person who rocked it while it was empty will most likely be the victim.

As with most superstitions, this one relies heavily on our fear that things we cannot begin to understand are always lying in wait, hoping for the opportunity to sever the tenuous thread that keeps us tethered to this realm. Apparently, all these insidious beings need in order to claim unsuspecting souls is for someone to open a door and invite them in. Rocking an empty chair is just one of these means to an end.

Should this costly mistake occur, there is a way to head off doom, but the guilty party needs to act quickly. In order to counteract the curse that has been set in motion, the one responsible must plant themselves in the chair and loudly recite a prayer in the name of the person whose life they have placed in jeopardy. If done correctly, this will ward off any soul collectors that may have been summoned by their careless actions.

It can't be stressed enough that, once the process has begun, only the person who rocked the chair in the first place can put things right. The safest means of avoiding such an ordeal is to simply be mindful of where we lay our hands. If a chair is meant to be rocked, make sure that someone is sitting in it while it is in motion.

When a person survives an automobile accident, it is truly a blessing. Afterwards, they go on with their lives, thankful for every day they have been given. What many don't know is that, according to lore, when a car that has been wrecked is deemed roadworthy following a devastating event, it carries with it a stigma that cannot be erased.

Supposedly, a vehicle that has been mangled in a road mishap was marked by fate. Something, somewhere, tried and failed to put it out of commission. The owner of such an automobile will find out soon enough that it will only be a matter of time before another accident finishes the job.

Surprisingly, this is one of the few bits of irrationalities that my family did not adhere to. I have heard it many times over the years, but not from any of my relatives. One source was an elderly gentleman who used to do minor repairs on my car out of his home garage. His name was Charlie.

Years ago, I purchased a used car from a dealership and took it to Charlie for a quick inspection. It should be noted that I knew nothing of the vehicle's history on the day I drove it into his garage.

The old man took one look at the car, a Ford Escort, and shook his head. A quick glance had told him that it had been wrecked at some point. He let me know in no uncertain terms that the vehicle was no good. I assumed that he meant that it wasn't mechanically sound, but as it turned out, that had not been the case.

Charlie was normally a man of few words, but he gave me an earful that day. He said that he didn't see anything wrong with the car, per se, but that I should take it back to the salesman and ask to see another model. He wiped his face with his hands as he advised me to get rid of the car as soon as possible.

I listened politely to what he had to say, even though his advice was going in one ear and out the other. I had just bought the car and had no intention of taking it back to the dealership. After he said his peace, I paid him for his trouble and went on my way without a care in the world.

Less than two weeks later, I was rear-ended while on my way home from work. As a result, I suffered whiplash that left me with excruciating headaches for many years to come. For its part, the car was deemed a total loss.

Perhaps Charlie's warning and the subsequent collision were merely coincidental. Whatever the case, I have always wondered if he knew a little bit more about cars than what could be seen under the hood.

It isn't clear where the rule of three got its start, but the notion that tragedies tend to occur in sequences of three has been around for centuries. Other numbers bring with them various superstitions; for instance, lucky number seven or the dreaded unlucky thirteen. None, however, can compete with the power of three.

The idea has been floated that the basis for three carrying with it a greater burden than other numerals is at least partially due to its association with the Holy Trinity. One of the more well-known examples of this is the belief that a match used to light three distinct objects, usually cigarettes or candles, is a defilement of the Father, Son and Holy Spirit.

SUPERSTITIONS, OLD WIVES' TALES, & FOLKLORE

The thought process behind this is that a source of fire is a powerful entity in and of itself. To utilize it three times in quick succession is to mock its power. Such a transgression invites misfortune into the life of the one who lit the match. The object of fate's wrath will go on to lead an existence fraught with hardship. When the time comes for them to meet their maker, the target of the spiritual attack is sent to their ultimate destination: the fires of Hell.

Most people are familiar with the claim that celebrity deaths come in threes. To be considered victims of the rule of three, their deaths must come within ten days of one another. It does happen, as in the case of Michael Jackson, Farrah Fawcett, and Ed McMahon who all died within days of each other in 2009. Likewise, Alan Thicke, George Michael, and Carrie Fisher also passed away in rapid succession in December of 2016.

Of course, the circle of life is constantly in motion, even for the most famous among us. The fact that, sometimes, their deaths occur in clusters could simply be coincidence. Then again, it could also indicate that the curse of three shows no mercy; even to those who lived otherwise charmed lives.

Airline disasters are also famous for occurring in this fateful sequence. In July of 2014, Malaysia Airlines Flight MH17, TransAsia Flight 222, and Air Algerie MD83 all went down in the span of one deadly week. Nearly five hundred lives were lost as a result.

In March of 2019, over the course of one weekend, three planes crashed in different parts of the world, killing one hundred seventy-four passengers in total. In the past two decades, there have only been three years (ironically) that didn't see a series of three plane crashes occurring within less than two weeks of each other.

We will probably never really know where the number three got its bad reputation. One wonders what makes three a charm as opposed to five or six. Why is knocking three times considered standard? Why did Dorothy have to click her heels together three times in order to return home? Wherever the answers lie, at some point, someone, somewhere decided that the number three would stand out from the rest as both a symbol of luck and of grave misfortune.

Salt, and the power it possesses, features prominently in folklore and old wives' tales. It is common knowledge that if we accidently knock over the salt shaker, the act must be followed by throwing a pinch of what was spilt over our left shoulder. This ritual is carried out in order to fend off the demon that has been summoned as a result of our careless action. Tossing salt into the face of the devil's cohort is said to send it back to the netherworld from whence it came.

Salt has held the distinction of being a protective device against evil spirits for centuries. In the Old World, it was believed that sprinkling salt around entryways would prevent untoward spirits from gaining access to occupied dwellings. This stemmed from the idea that nothing sent from the depths of Hell could cross an unbroken line of salt.

In the days when witches were thought to be hiding around every corner, salt was used to deter them from preying upon villagers. In an attempt to keep these night hunters occupied once the sun went down, mounds of salt were often poured outside of homes. Since it was believed that witches couldn't pass salt without counting every grain, this method was used to keep them busy until daybreak.

When the sun began to emerge on the horizon, the witch would be forced to retreat until nightfall when the entire process would be repeated. Thanks to their ingenuity, townspeople were able to go about their lives, confidant that they wouldn't fall victim to these wicked entities, at least until they ran out of salt.

Besides thwarting the purveyors of evil, salt was considered so valuable that it was used in lieu of currency in the times of ancient Rome. Soldiers, for instance, were sometimes paid for their services in salt. Since the element was considered a virtual cure-all, its various uses made it a coveted commodity. A natural preservative as well as a powerful disinfectant, salt was indispensable on the battlefield. It was also a source of sodium, a mineral essential to maintaining health and well-being.

Salt was so respected that to spill this precious resource was comparable to committing a mortal sin. Children grew up being warned that opportunistic demons lie in wait for just such an occurrence. Their wrath was the punishment one would face for being clumsy with that which was seen as priceless. After hearing that, it's understandable that even the most rambunctious youngster was careful not to waste a grain of what we now take for granted.

Churches even joined in to sing the praises of salt. Many religious establishments held it in the same esteem as holy water for its power to ward off evil. Salt was viewed as such a symbol of purity that even the most pious worshippers believed in the sanctity of the tiny grains. So untouchable was salt that it was oftentimes sprinkled on the bodies of the dead prior to burial to act as a protectant in the afterlife.

Much like garlic to a vampire or kryptonite to Superman, salt is used to this day as a repellent for creatures that are condemned to the dark side. It is thought that demons and those with whom they hold court are repulsed by anything containing salt. Throughout the centuries, if a guest was invited to share a meal and refused to partake of any food that had been seasoned with salt, they were assumed to be witches or some other tool of the devil. It would appear that watching one's sodium intake in those days could prove to be their downfall.

Although salt has long been touted as an effective barrier against a wide variety of demonic entities, there are schools of thought that fly in the face of those traditional beliefs. Rather than boasting of the sanctity of salt, there are those who firmly believe that it attracts more evil than it repels. They maintain that any self-respecting demon could easily erase any traces of the substance and enter a home with a flick of their wrist. Just as what one person finds appalling another may relish, so it goes with the things that exist in the shadow realm.

A magic circle, also known as a witch's circle, often utilizes salt to form a protective barrier. This is considered a safe zone from anything bent on doing harm. Unfortunately, unless one is the creator of the circle, it is impossible to know if the safety net exists inside of the ring of salt or out. Only the practitioner holds the key and they are not about to share that information. In the end, those on the wrong side of the circle will soon find that they are powerless in the face of whatever tortures the purveyor has in store.

Salt has other uses that aren't at all frightening. For instance, some people believe that putting a sprinkling of salt inside your shoes will prompt a growth spurt. Rumor has it that, when he was very young, former Chicago Bulls superstar Michael Jordan's mother suggested that he try this age-old trick in an attempt to increase his height. If the account is true, it certainly worked. The basketball superstar ended up topping off at six feet, six inches tall.

Whether it is used for good, evil, or simply to season a spread of food, salt holds an indelible place in nearly every household across the globe. Possessing a rich history, the importance of this versatile condiment in our everyday lives is undeniable. So, the next time you add a pinch to your Sunday dinner, keep in mind that every tiny grain tells a tale.

SUPERSTITIONS, OLD WIVES' TALES, & FOLKLORE

Sources:
Folklore.usc.edu
Rod Serling and Earl Hamner Jr.-*The Hunt-1962*
Space.com
Facebook.com
Caringcardinals.com
Petsmagazine.com
Wikipedia.com
Appalachian Folklore
Protectthewhitedeer.com
Merriam-webster.com
Wideopencountry.com
Peoplehowstuffworks.com
Animalwised.com
Thegreatcat.org
Nypost.com
Learnreligions.com
Historic-uk.com
Bobvila.com
History.com
Animalfriends.co.uk
Britannica.com
Stuff.co.nz
Dot.asia
Washington Post.com
Quora.com
Mothership.sg
Huffpost.com
Sun-sentinel.com
Readers Digest.com
Theculturetrip.com
U.S. News

Koreaboo.com
Evilfandom.com
Smithsonianmag.com
Donald Dossey
Atlasobscura
Bustle.com
Up and Down With the Rolling Stones-Tony Sanchez-1979
Sciencefocus.com
The Search for Dracula-Echo Bridge Entertainment-1996
Pinterest.com
Gem-a.com
Jewelryshoppingguide.com
Mythencyclopedia.com
Housebeautiful.com

Acknowledgements

Thank you to my family for their unending support.

Thanks to those who instilled in me the love of folklore and superstition that I carry with me to this day.

Immeasurable respect and appreciation to those who read, and hopefully enjoy, my work. Your continued support means more than you will ever know.

The book Superstitions, Old Wives' Tales, & Folklore is the sole property of its author Cindy Parmiter.

Any unauthorized reproduction is strictly prohibited without the author's express written consent.

All rights reserved.

Copyright established June 2021.

Cover art licensed from and courtesy of Burmakin Andrey

Don't miss out!

Visit the website below and you can sign up to receive emails whenever Cindy Parmiter publishes a new book. There's no charge and no obligation.

https://books2read.com/r/B-A-DBDP-VBPPB

BOOKS 2 READ

Connecting independent readers to independent writers.

Did you love *Superstitions, Old Wives' Tales, & Folklore*? Then you should read *16 True Tales of Fear & Fright*[1] by Cindy Parmiter!

This book is brimming with accounts of brushes with the paranormal and unexplained that are sure to please readers looking for stories with a bit of bite. Included in this collection are true tales of ghostly encounters, a haunted hotel, an arachnophobe's worst nightmare that became terrifyingly real, inanimate objects that are rumored to come to life at will, a teenage girl's first taste of freedom that went horribly awry, run-ins with creatures of unknown origin, vengeful spirits that torment the living and much more. If it is a scare you seek, you've come to the right place.

---

1. https://books2read.com/u/bQyZKv
2. https://books2read.com/u/bQyZKv

Also by Cindy Parmiter

In The Realm of the Eerie & Unexplained
In The Realm of the Eerie & Unexplained: Volume 2
In the Realm of the Eerie & Unexplained: Volume 3

Standalone
In The Realm Of The Eerie & Unexplained
True Stories From The Dark Side: Volume 1
Truly Twisted Bedtime Stories
Chilling Tales From The Shadowlands
Superstitions, Old Wives' Tales, & Folklore
The Horror Of Skinned Tom & Other Spooky Tales
True Scares And Real-Life Nightmares
True Scares And Real-Life Nightmares: Volume 2
True Tales of the Paranormal, Mysterious & Macabre
Tales Too Strange To Be Fiction
Fear of the Night: Real Tales of Sleep Paralysis, Night Terrors, & Prophetic Dreams
True Ghostly Tales: Hauntings
The Wretched One & Other True Spine-Tingling Tales
16 True Tales of Fear & Fright
The True Stories Behind Your Favorite Fairy Tales & Nursery Rhymes
True Scares and Real-Life Nightmares: The Collection

True Stories of the Paranormal: The Complete Collection
True Tales of the Supernatural & Unexplained: Volume 2
Urban Legends: The Collection

www.ingramcontent.com/pod-product-compliance
Ingram Content Group UK Ltd.
Pitfield, Milton Keynes, MK11 3LW, UK
UKHW041436160126
10147UKWH00029B/152